Praise for *More Than Money*

"Forget the textbooks, this is what happens in the real world. Life is messy and unpredictable—this book tells stories of how to deal with it."
—Morgan Housel, author of *The Psychology of Money*

"Justin Castelli and Taylor Schulte have used their superpowers to assemble an instant classic anthology. This collection of ideas from America's up-and-coming class of talented advisors has something for everyone."
—Downtown Josh Brown, CEO of Ritholtz Wealth Management and star of CNBC's The Halftime Report

"Money is power ... the hard part is aligning that power with what's actually important to us. That's a journey, and this is a guidebook."
—Carl Richards, author of *The Behavior Gap*

"Financial planning is not just about numbers. In *More Than Money* Advisors Growing as a Community shows how impactful and lifechanging financial planning can be. The collection of stories in the book are a testament to how advisors can help clients unleash the power within and see new possibilities."
—Luis F. Rosa, CFP® EA, co-founder of BLatinX Internship

"From planning a young family's future, to launching a new business venture, to regaining control after life's unexpected events, these stories show the power of partnering with advisors who have the vision to share your dreams and the expertise to connect the pieces of your financial puzzle to optimize your chances of success. As you read, you will get a glimpse into the deeper impact of real financial planning."
—Perth Tolle, founder, Life + Liberty Indexes

MORE
THAN
MONEY

MORE THAN MONEY

Real-Life Stories of Financial Planning

Edited by

SHANNA DUE

Curated by

TAYLOR SCHULTE

JUSTIN CASTELLI

 Harriman House

HARRIMAN HOUSE LTD
3 Viceroy Court
Bedford Road
Petersfield
Hampshire
GU32 3LJ
GREAT BRITAIN
Tel: +44 (0)1730 233870

Email: enquiries@harriman-house.com
Website: harriman.house

First published in 2023.
Copyright © The AGC

Paperback ISBN: 978-0-85719-990-4
eBook ISBN: 978-0-85719-991-1

British Library Cataloguing in Publication Data
A CIP catalogue record for this book can be obtained from the British Library.

CONTENTS

FOREWORD BY CHRISTINE BENZ

FOR YEARS, TUNING into HGTV has been one of my favorite guilty pleasures when I've found myself in charge of my household's remote control and I've wanted to turn my brain off for a bit. And the guiltiest pleasure of all is a program called *My Lottery Dream Home*. The premise is simple: With the help of a charming celebrity real estate expert, the new lottery winners shop for the house they've always longed for, which they're finally able to afford thanks to their recent windfall.

For these newly minted millionaires, their vision of what having wealth means is invariably a bit of a caricature: a sprawling home with more bedrooms than they're likely to use, an impressive swimming pool for entertaining family and friends, and a huge garage to store multiple expensive cars and boats. No one asks them to go any deeper, to delve into how money might transform their lives in more substantive ways. That's not the point of the show.

That *is* the point of the book that you're holding, though—even though it's about regular people rather than overnight millionaires. The financial planners who have contributed essays to *More Than Money* know that real wealth is about so much more than outward shows of "we made it!" While most of us do, in fact, cherish the idea of living in a beautiful, peaceful home, that's because home is the place where we raise our children, gather with friends, and put up our feet to watch HGTV after a challenging workday. When we say that having a beautiful home is important to us, we're probably saying we want much more than that.

In each of the essays that follow, financial planners share real-life stories of how they helped their clients uncover what gives them meaning and purpose, then worked to align their finances to support that vision. For these planners, the careful implementation of the financial plan—the investment selection, the tax planning, the insurance coverage, the spreadsheeting that we associate with financial professionals—is crucial. But it's also, in the words of financial planner Michael Kelly, "table stakes"—the bare minimum that a client should expect from working with a qualified financial planner. Even more important is the work that precedes it, the discovery process that good-quality financial planners employ to help clients get to the bottom of their "why" and to understand what's possible in their lives.

You'll read stories of working parents coming to grips with the fact that the financial rewards of their breakneck schedules aren't worth the time away from their growing kids, and widows charting a way forward following the sudden passing of their spouses. You'll hear about entrepreneurs who are articulating their next act after a lifetime of nurturing their businesses and married couples aiming to get on the same page with their money. You'll probably see some of your own story reflected in this book's pages.

Along the way, you'll come away with some practical financial planning ideas for tackling your own money challenges and improving your own plan. And I'm pretty sure you'll be inspired, not just to improve your financial allocations but what I call your "time on Earth" allocations, too. I know that I was.

Happy reading!

Christine Benz
Director of personal finance and retirement planning,
Morningstar, Inc.

INTRODUCTION

There is the textbook answer and then there is
YOUR answer.

— *Taylor Schulte, CFP®*

I T IS A common misconception that financial planning is all about spreadsheets and numbers. As Taylor regularly reminds listeners on the *Stay Wealthy Retirement Podcast*, that belief could not be further from the truth.

While there is a textbook answer for every financial decision, it may not always be the right answer for the individual. Real financial planning is a balance between the values of the individual and the spreadsheet. Real financial planning is more art than science.

What better way to show you the art behind real financial planning than from authentic stories from real financial advisors?

Welcome to *More Than Money*. This is Justin Castelli and Taylor Schulte here to greet you, as you join us for a peek into 28 real-life stories gleaned from our community's most inspiring financial planning experiences.

REAL-LIFE STORIES,
REAL-LIFE RELATIONSHIPS

From a couple nearing retirement, only to hit an unexpected roadblock; to a divorced professional with a cryptocurrency fortune, but cash-flow challenges; to a young widow rebuilding a new course in life for herself—each of these true stories represent day-in-the-life snapshots from 28 clients who were willing to share their most profound financial experiences with you.

Each of their stories is a gift from a brave soul (although all names and some particulars have been changed to protect their privacy). After all, most of us are reluctant to talk about our money among friends and family, let alone in public. But these clients—from individuals, to couples, to family dynasties—agreed to let us share their truths, to help others just like you think through similar questions of your own. We owe a debt of gratitude to each of them.

We believe you'll find inspiration in each tale. Which brings us to the theme behind *More Than Money: Real-life Stories of Financial Planning*.

THE POWER TO...

Do you find yourself feeling overpowered by money? Or have you optimized your financial resources to empower *you*? Whether you prefer to operate independently or hire a financial advisor, what will it take for you to take charge of your financial independence, come what may?

It helps to embark with a financial plan, to shape your informed and intentional choices about your money. But then what? The money is meaningless if it doesn't grant you the power to live your best life.

That's why we've organized our *More Than Money* tales of financial planning by the greater forces we experience throughout our lives. Each chapter includes a collection of personal anecdotes that speak to an important empowerment:

- The power to work and to play.
- The power to change and to preserve.
- The power to celebrate and to grieve.
- The power of family and of independence.
- The power to give and to receive.

WHO IS AGC?

How, you may wonder, did this whole project get started?

You might say the story behind *More Than Money* began about 20 years ago when Justin was a high school student in Indianapolis, Indiana:

> My 11th grade teacher Ms. Fischer had an interesting tradition she called 'Pass the Fisch.' These sessions were a safe space for students to share what was going on in their lives. I never really had any huge problems to get off my chest, but it was nice to know there was a place for us to unload if we needed to. Many of my fellow students did use the sessions to talk about some pretty heavy stuff, and it helped bring us closer together as a group, with lasting lessons I am still thankful for today.

Fast forward to a few years ago, when Taylor and I were swapping ideas about our respective practices. We talked about how, like anyone else, no financial advisor does their best work by operating from an island. We wanted to form our own version of Pass the Fisch.

As Taylor describes it:

> Early in my career, I would reach out to other advisors I respected, sometimes driving hours to meet them for lunch and a conversation. I wouldn't be where I am today without being able to learn from generous peers who took my calls and agreed to meet with a random stranger. Knowing how instrumental this was for me (but how awkward it can feel to contact people out of the blue), I dreamed of creating a forum for those of us who prefer to view our peers as collaborators, not competitors.

In 2019, we co-founded **Advisors Growing as a Community**, or **AGC**, as a private online network for financial advisors who want to collaborate with professional peers who:

- Recognize that personal development is just as important as professional development.

  If I can continue to grow and learn how to be a better person, friend, husband, father, and son, I believe I will naturally become a better advisor to my clients.

  — *Taylor Schulte*

- Exhibit an abundance mentality, embracing opportunities to elevate others without expecting anything in return.

  Historically, our profession has been a cut-throat exchange in which it's every advisor for themselves. It's inspiring to be part of a community coming together to exchange technical expertise, offer moral support, and even refer clients to one another.

  — *Justin Castelli*

- Have a passion for learning, growing, and improving every day.

  Our mission is to provide a safe, collaborative space for advisors to learn and grow alongside their peers.

  — *The AGC website*

In short, AGC members regularly lean on one another. From collaborating to solve real-life planning scenarios, to applauding professional milestones, to empathizing over personal setbacks—if we can help one another become better as advisors and as people, we believe we can better serve our clients and make a lasting impact in our communities.

A BOOK IS BORN

But let's get back to *More Than Money*.

While we are responsible for getting the AGC ball rolling, we never could have imagined how far and fast its members would run with it… including coming together to publish this remarkable book!

In true AGC spirit, we will be donating all net proceeds from the book to non-profit financial planning organizations such as the Foundation for Financial Planning (FFP), and BLatinX Internship Program (BLX).

As you peruse its pages, you'll meet many of the advisors in our community. Each chapter is authored by an AGC member who volunteered their time and talents to contribute their part to the whole. We salute you all, and congratulate you as now-published authors!

We would be remiss if we didn't give special credit to AGC member Shanna Due. As project leader, Shanna sacrificed countless hours to organize, encourage, inspire, and occasionally nudge us, as we pressed forward on a painfully tight deadline. We also would like to thank Mallory Clouse, the AGC Community Manager. Without her dedication and commitment to our thriving membership, projects like this would not be possible. Finally, we want to acknowledge and thank Carl Richards and Wendy Cook for their objective counsel and creative contributions, as well as our publisher, Harriman House, for helping us realize our vision. While these colleagues aren't AGC members, they are indeed kindred spirits.

We'd like to wrap with an empowering tale from Justin's own experiences as an advisor:

> One of my most memorable moments as a financial advisor was helping a very special client retire 10 years earlier than she thought possible. Turns out, it totally was, thanks to her years of diligent saving and stalwart investing. I'd like to think my advice along

the way helped too. Showing her the big picture and stress-testing different scenarios gave her the confidence she needed to let go of a career she had loved, but was ready to move beyond. As friends visited her in her new home and rejuvenated life, they began to rethink their own finances as well. 'Thanks!' she recently said to me, 'You've given me 10 years of my life back!'

That client? If you haven't guessed it yet, it's Justin's 11th grade teacher, Ms. Fischer.

THE POWER
TO WORK

THE GIFT OF TIME

Michael Kelly, CFA, CFP®

Michael Kelly, CFA, CFP® is the founder and president of Switchback Financial, a fee-only financial planning firm based in Madison, CT. After a decade-long career in Treasury and Capital Management at some of the world's largest banks, Michael decided that helping bolster the bottom line of the big corporations was not providing happiness and meaning to his life and decided it was time for a change. Frustrated by seeing colleagues and friends struggle with the overly complex world of personal finance, he realized that a more purposeful path was to educate and guide peers through managing their hard-earned money.

Michael specifically focuses on helping young professionals/families with equity compensation deal with the investment management, tax planning, and behavioral complexities that stem from concentrated positions. His purpose is to empower individuals to make sound financial decisions based on their core values to live a balanced life—enjoying a fulfilling life today without sacrificing their future.

WEIGHT OF UNKNOWNS

Like most of my clients, Josh and Christina were young professionals—at least young in terms of those who are often engaging with financial planners.

They were both late 30-somethings, with two children, a home, and each with a well-paying job. Both had come up through the technology industry and worked their way up to senior management roles at their respective companies. Neither were sitting in c-suite positions, but they had prominent roles with solid pay and significant responsibility. Additionally, they both were relatively conservative regarding spending and debt—especially Josh.

Great jobs, ownership of a beautiful home, and solid foundations when it came to spending and saving—I'm sure you are asking yourself what problem they could have possibly been facing.

In terms of pure numbers, there wasn't anything significant. Things were solid in most of the critical areas. The problem is that Josh and Christina lacked confidence in their decision-making. They had a gut feeling that they had done a decent job handling their money, but both still had an underlying fear that they were making mistakes and not taking full advantage of opportunities. They, like many others, reached out to me because the weight of these unknowns brought them to the point of realizing things were beyond their knowledge base, and they didn't have the time to do the research themselves.

WHEN TIME MEANS
MORE THAN MONEY

This scenario is extremely common with many of the folks I work with.

The individuals have worked hard to get to a stable place in life, but their time has become a scarcer resource than money as their careers have developed. Taking it upon themselves to learn how to best handle their given financial situations simply eats into more of their valuable time. It is at this point that they face one of three routes:

1. They feel that things are good enough and merely move forward with the status quo, unaware of opportunities missed or threats lingering.
2. They decide to tackle the problem head-on and allocate time to educate themselves on how to maximize their dollars instead of dedicating that limited time toward family, friends, or hobbies.
3. They understand that they don't want or need to take on a second career of managing their own money, but also know it needs to be addressed. Therefore, they begin working with a financial expert.

Josh and Christina chose the third route, and from the moment we sat down for an introduction, they were open-minded and willing to partner.

FINDING THEIR "WHY"

Before we even talked about numbers, investments, or accounts, we had a discussion about what really matters—their "why."

We talked about what they were looking to get out of life and what brings them happiness. You see, money is merely a tool and should not be the goal. If used properly, this tool can help propel us to achieve what we truly value in life and get us to that point of contentment we are all looking to achieve.

With Josh and Christina, it was evident from everything we discussed that the things they held highest were family and security. Yet, they were both on the verge of burnout in their careers, openly admitted that they had golden handcuffs, and were working too many hours at the office. Things weren't totally off track to the point that they were ready to walk away from their paychecks, but as I gently pressed further, it was clear that they each had ideas for where they ideally wanted to take their careers.

Christina's dream scenario had been shared and discussed before, and it was not totally out of left field. She admitted that she didn't want to keep operating in the manner in which she was currently. She never felt like she was making a real impact with her work. She felt that going out on her own and consulting for start-up firms was a potentially viable path if she could ever get over the fear of the initial leap of faith. The issue was that she constantly felt tied to her job because of her equity compensation. The annual influx of company stock kept holding her back from ever executing on her passion, no matter how put together her plan was. She thought that making such a drastic change would also mean making a significant change in the family's lifestyle and drastically impacting her and Josh's retirement.

Josh's scenario came as a bit of a revelation. The long hours and constant fire drills were starting to take a toll. He admitted that he was unsure how much longer he could keep going in the same capacity. He dreamed of slowly pulling back on his responsibilities over time and being more present in their kids' activities. He enjoyed the people he worked with and his projects, but the constant stress of being the lead was wearing him down. He even shared that someday if they were financially able, he would love to quit and pursue a lower-paying role in the fitness industry. This received a bit of a laugh from Christina and even himself, but his admission was rooted in truth.

IMPACT BEYOND THE BASICS

Following our deeper conversation, we got to work and began crafting their financial plan. We were able to highlight their strengths when it came to budgeting and debt management. We identified how great their savings rate was and highlighted that there were no mistakes with their investments – only methods to improve them. Through our review, we also spotlighted opportunities to save significant money by refinancing their mortgage, reducing risk by buying private life insurance, and even the benefits of implementing a tax-efficient path for handling Christina's equity compensation. Finally, we developed a more optimal method for their investments to better match their unique risk/return profile, all at a lower cost than they were paying.

In my opinion, though, that is merely table stakes. That is what any decent planner operating as a fiduciary should be doing. Nothing within the plan was overly complex or complicated.

What had the most significant impact for Josh and Christina was that we were able to build a scenario within their plan to show how chasing their dreams wasn't as far a stretch as they thought. We even developed a case in which we made the dramatic change of reducing both of their incomes by 25%, and the results showed that it would not force them to make lifestyle changes nor put them at significant risk in retirement. Seeing real evidence (even if still assumption-based) that their dream life was there for the taking was beyond powerful.

THE ULTIMATE GOAL

Now to answer the question on your mind: no, Josh and Christina didn't see their plan and go hand in their resignations the next day, or even the next month.

They are both still working for their same employers and in their same capacities, for now. But as we went through the dream scenario of their plan in the presentation meeting, you could see a lightening of their faces. You could sense the stress from the feeling of being trapped being released when they could see that there was a way out. They expressed how nice it was to know that they weren't stuck on the proverbial treadmill until they hit 65 and could retire. The golden handcuffs released at least a few notches, and they felt they had a bit more power in their life.

This is the true value a planner can add. The dollars earned from solid investment choices, or the savings gained from implementing tax strategies, are all good reasons to work with an expert.

But the real reason why I believe working with a professional is so important is that an effective planner can help individuals tap into themselves and discover pathways they are too in the weeds to envision.

An effective planner serves as a guide that partners in reframing money as an effective tool in creating your best life and not as an obstacle or weight preventing it. It's not merely about the intellectual quotient (IQ) of the planner, but it's about their emotional quotient (EQ) that enables them to relate to their clients and get them motivated to take action.

PLANNING CAN HELP ALL

Finally, people love to tell stories of the underdogs—how individuals utilized grit and determination to beat seemingly insurmountable odds and become extreme successes. We all love to hear these tales as well. Sports fan or not, we all have heard about Michael Jordan getting cut from his high school basketball team to then go on to be the greatest player of all time.

Hearing powerful success stories can be inspirational and motivating. However, some may read these stories and think, "But my situation isn't the anomaly." They may think they aren't the outlier, and therefore that positive outcome can't possibly happen for them. Or, in the case of the stories in this book, they may believe there isn't an opportunity for them to work with a planner and have the results make an impactful and significant change in their lives.

That is why it's important to share how great planning goes beyond the numbers and is about helping clients gain enough confidence to reduce the everyday stress that money can have.

I hope that the story of Josh and Christina can help people relate and realize you don't have to have extraneous circumstances to have amazing outcomes.

IN SUMMARY

- Money is merely a tool and should not be the goal. If used properly, this tool can help propel us to achieve what we truly value in life and get us to that point of contentment.
- Solid financial planning is valuable at all income levels.

A LIGHTHOUSE IN THE STORM

Christopher Clepp

Christopher Clepp is a financial planner with Strategic Financial Group, a fee-based financial planning practice in the West Loop of Chicago, who focuses on helping business owners between the ages of 35 and 55 make work optional.

Christopher Clepp is a registered representative, offering securities through The O.N. Equity Sales Company, Member FINRA/SIPC, One Financial Way Cincinnati, Oh. 45242, 513 794-6794. Investment advisory services offered through O.N. Investment Management Company.

I'm tired of feeling like I'm in an ocean with huge waves all around me and no one to help me through the storm.

—Mary

WHEN I MET Mary at a business incubator event, she proved herself to be a brilliant business owner who loves what she does. She was smart and funny, but also passionate about running her business ethically and "giving back" to the people who worked for her.

After we chatted for a while, Mary confided in me that she wanted an outside opinion on her personal and business finances. As the head of a growing company in a competitive field, she had been juggling her business, supporting her aging parents, and trying to take care of herself while ensuring a comfortable future. Unfortunately, she was feeling stretched rather thin, and she knew she wasn't devoting the time required to plot out the future she wanted.

During my first conversation with Mary, we talked for more than 90 minutes without the normal formalities or any documents to go over. She told me about a negative experience she had with a financial advisor in the past who had made her feel small and inadequate—feelings she was unaccustomed to having as a commanding force in her field.

After she felt comfortable enough to share more, she told me she wanted help with the financial side of her life—not because she wasn't capable, but because she knew it was smart to call in professional help so she could focus on running her company.

I feel fortunate Mary trusted me enough to let me help her plan the future she really wanted. From there, our real work began.

BALANCING PROFITS WITH PASSION AND RESPONSIBILITY

Unlike some corporate CEOs and business owners, Mary had always strived to achieve a balance between pursuing success and gaining wealth while upholding her core values. She was emotionally invested in the success of her company, but she was equally committed to the success of the people who worked for her, some of whom had devoted their entire adult lives to helping her business grow.

Unfortunately, she had focused so much of her efforts on this balancing act that she had neglected some important aspects of her own life. Mary hadn't opened a retirement account or started a plan for her employees. She had also overlooked her need to set up a finely tuned succession plan for her business that would kick in once she was ready to retire.

Mary had also taken on some major caretaking responsibilities for her aging parents, and she wanted to ensure they would be okay no matter what. During our meetings, her concern for her parents was palpable. Her dad had retired from a company without receiving the pension he was promised, and now her parents faced a retirement that did not live up to their long-held dreams.

She knew that, if something happened to her at that exact moment, such as death or disability, her parents could be left to figure out an uncertain future on their own. That was something that Mary couldn't live with, and it was probably the main driver that led her to seek out a financial advisor at that point. She had been working to build a successful business for decades, but she didn't have a backup plan for life's many "what ifs."

Finally, Mary wanted a fresh perspective on where to take her business. Her company was where all of her wealth originated from, and she wanted to make sure she wasn't missing out on ways to grow her revenue and increase her margins while recruiting, retaining and enriching the lives of her employees.

Ultimately, our conversation made me realize Mary had a complete vision for what she wanted in her life. She just needed to put the systems in place that would help her get there.

Throughout our conversations, Mary wanted to have the following questions answered:

- What steps could she take to ensure the financial future she wanted—both for herself and for her parents?
- What was the best way to help her employees save for retirement?
- How could she support causes that brought her satisfaction and joy while also increasing profits?
- Also, what was the "magic number" she should shoot for in terms of invested assets before she could retire?

Looking over the full picture of what Mary was dealing with, it was no wonder she felt surrounded by all those huge waves.

PLANNING FOR THE PRESENT AND THE FUTURE

After many conversations with Mary, it was easy to identify her primary goals. She wanted to organize her financial life, continue to care for her parents, and be able to grow and sell her business to her employees in 10 to 15 years. She also wanted to set up a separate retirement plan for herself and her employees, and to make sure she had an adequate amount of insurance in place for each aspect of her life.

Once in retirement, she also wanted to travel and continue supporting causes she believed in. Mary *did not* want to retire and live on a tight fixed budget for the rest of her life, and can you blame her?

As part of our planning process, I also wound up having several conversations with Mary's mentor and her accountant. This was partially so I could access the financial figures I needed, but also so we could all work together from the same playbook.

During our group conversations, Mary wound up having an epiphany about another aspect of her life she probably needed help with. In addition to hiring a financial planner to take on the grunt work of planning her financial future, she also needed to hire a CFO for her business.

Ideally, Mary said she would love to hire a woman for the role. Her history in a male-dominated industry in corporate America showed her how often women were passed over for promotions, acknowledgements, and equitable pay.

As a business owner who wanted to align her company's values with her own, this move made total sense. Fortunately, she found the perfect fit for her company within a matter of weeks, and that new hire enabled Mary to increase margins, explore new opportunities and ensure her company would continue to live in alignment with her values long after she was gone.

Once Mary had outsourced this important work, she was able to focus on the planning process even more. Steps we took to ensure her financial success include:

- **Setting up a will and estate plan:** Mary wanted to make sure her parents were taken care of in every scenario, including her own untimely death. Since she hadn't yet set up a will or an estate plan, she sat down with an estate planning attorney to get those important documents taken care of.
- **Protecting against life's "what ifs":** Since Mary's income was dependent on her continuing to run her business, she knew she needed to protect her parents in case her income disappeared. She bought several types of insurance coverage to provide peace of mind.
- **Setting up an investing plan based on Mary's risk tolerance and timeline:** She had two accounts from previous corporate engagements that were invested in target-date funds. While the investments themselves were not exceptionally poor for her situation, they were not invested in a way that aligned with her values. Ultimately, we moved Mary's money under management and put it through a stock selection process to make sure it was invested in companies she could support.
- **Opening a retirement plan for Mary:** Finally, Mary opened a retirement account that would let her fund her retirement goals with as many tax advantages as possible. This step was long overdue, but our calculations showed she still had plenty of time to build the wealth she needed to enjoy her golden years. During this part of the process, we also nailed down the amount of money Mary needed to save and invest each month to reach her goals.

In addition to the steps we took for Mary, she also wanted to set her employees up for success. We looked at expanding the benefits offered to employees, including health insurance. We also helped set up retirement plans for her employees that included matching funds and other benefits from the company.

WHEN THE PANDEMIC HIT...

Shortly after we brought Mary's money under our management, COVID-19 reared its ugly head and the market crash of 2020 hit. The entire ordeal was stressful for everyone. However, Mary's financial plan was carefully crafted for every situation, including this one. There was nothing—not even a pandemic—that was going to change her course of action.

While plenty of people were panicking, Mary told me it was easier to remain calm in the market knowing her investments were with companies that aligned with her values. It also helped that she had a plan built around her investing timeline and long-term goals, all of which hadn't changed just because COVID-19 had upended all our lives. After all, her investing strategy was built with all kinds of market scenarios in mind—for the good times and the bad.

Mary was right; it *is* considerably easier to stay focused on long-term goals when those goals are clearly laid out and you have a comprehensive financial plan to support them.

Fortunately, we all know what happened after that. After some crazy stock market movements that lasted for months, the markets rebounded and settled down. Now Mary's investments are doing better than ever, which is only possible because she trusted the plan she made and stayed the course.

PLOTTING YOUR COURSE TO RETIREMENT

Imagine you're on a boat over troubled waters, and that you have an idea of what your destination looks like, but you aren't sure how to get there. That's where Mary found herself several years ago, and yes, she was surrounded by waves coming from every direction. Without a beacon of light to follow or a map to get her where she was going, she felt completely lost.

During a recent client check-in call, Mary told me she doesn't feel so alone in the ocean anymore. Her financial plan has become a lighthouse and a guide for her to follow, and she loves knowing help is always nearby.

More importantly, Mary no longer spends sleepless nights wondering if she is on track with retirement and other financial goals. Instead of worrying how the next few decades might unfold, she is able to focus on running her business—what she had hoped to be able to do all along.

In my opinion, that's as good as it gets in the world of financial planning. We don't know what's coming, what the stock market returns will be, or what kind of roadblocks we'll face on the road to the future we want. But with a financial road map in place, we can focus our energy on other aspects of our lives and know that *all* of life's "what ifs"—including a worldwide pandemic—are planned for.

IN SUMMARY

- Don't be afraid to call on professional financial help, so you can focus on running your company.
- It is considerably easier to stay focused on long-term goals when those goals are clearly laid out and you have a comprehensive financial plan to support them.

CORPORATE RELEASE VALVE

Vincent R. Barbera

Vincent Barbera was born in the suburbs of Philadelphia. He had a passion for two things: being an entrepreneur, and helping others. As a young boy, he created different ventures, including neighborhood candy stores, lawn care business, and cable man. He took that love of finance and helping people and majored in psychology and business as an undergrad at the University of Pittsburgh. He would go on to earn his CFP® certification and a master's degree in finance from St Joseph's University. This education provided the pathway for him to start Newbridge Wealth Management with Chris Wiegand. Here he can pursue both of his passions: owning a business, and providing people peace of mind around their financial life. Prior to this, Vincent started his career at The Vanguard Group in the early 2000s. After about five years he felt a hollow feeling that continued to grow bigger every waking day. He knew he needed to make a change to save himself and to control his own financial freedom. Vincent now works with individuals who are experiencing similar pain points and he empowers them to secure their own financial futures. Vincent does this with smart financial planning and a keen understanding of the underlying psychological effects of making such a change.

"**I**s it just me, or are the leaves less vibrant this year?"

Coming from anyone else, I might have politely agreed or disagreed, and moved on. Pleasant small talk.

But this was Bob, and this wasn't the kind of question he usually asks. Bob takes daily walks in the woods behind his house, and marvels at every tiny new discovery made.

"See what I mean?" added his wife, Sandy. "Bob's job is compromising our family's soul."

It was then I knew that this generally jovial couple in their late 40s—think a young Mr. and Mrs. Santa Claus—needed to talk about more than autumn leaves and fall financial statements that day back in 2015.

How do you escape the corporate rat race, embark on a more satisfying career path, and (hopefully) not go broke? Walk with me, and I'll tell you the story of Bob and Sandy Burke, who were stuck in a rut, and needed to plan anew.

A SCARY, EXCITING LEAP OF FAITH

Let's begin at the end. By combining targeted coaching with detailed business, financial, tax, and retirement planning, the Burkes were able to become their own bosses, and regain the color in their life. Today, they're considering selling their thriving business within a few years and moving into a well-funded retirement.

However, if you're thinking of changing up your own career, be forewarned: If you want to land on your feet, you need to put in a lot of planning. And even then, life happens. The personal and financial risks are real, and happily-ever-after endings are not guaranteed. As Bob said when we were about to implement their exciting, unnerving plan: "Okay, it's time to take control … with fingers crossed."

INTRODUCING THE BURKES

Let us return to 2015. At the time, I'd been Bob and Sandy's advisor for close to 10 years. Bob was vice president of sales for an elevator company called Metalworks. Sandy was trained as a Registered Nurse but hadn't worked in a few years. They had two teenage kids, Elizabeth and Nicholas. I loved how the entire family made a point of spending quality time together. They enjoyed hiking in Vermont and skiing at Stowe Mountain. One of their lifetime goals was to visit all the national parks in the country.

Oh, and Bob's big belly laughs really did go, "Ho, ho, ho."

At the time, the Burkes' annual income was generous, and their retirement savings were comfortable. But was "generous" and "comfortable" worth it if it meant Bob had lost his laugh?

THE ALL-HANDS FAMILY GOAL MEETING

It was high time to revisit the Burkes' past assumptions in what I call an "All-Hands Family Goal Meeting." All cards and every feeling are laid on the table for inspection, including financial assumptions and emotional impacts.

Sandy opened the meeting with an emphatic, "Bob needs out." Frustration rolled off her in waves as she described how unhappy he'd grown with his career. With continual restructuring, he'd had five different managers in fewer years, scant job security, and no true love for what he did. After 20 years with Metalworks, he just didn't feel appreciated anymore.

I looked over at Bob. He was nodding in agreement, but his head was down.

After a pause, he looked up and sighed, "I don't know if we can afford to make such a big change at this point in our lives. What if we're stuck?"

You see, Bob was faced with a problem many private company

corporate executives share. Most of his assets were in tax-deferred accounts, such as rollover IRAs and 401(k) plans. For Bob to raise cash for a career transition, there would be tax consequences as well as potential penalties if he were to withdraw retirement money too soon. Sandy had the same problem. Since she had been a nurse for a large hospital, her money was in a rollover IRA as well. Between them, they only had about $40,000 in non-retirement cash reserves.

GETTING UNSTUCK

"Let's set aside the financials for a moment," I suggested. "What do you really *want* to do?"

Answering that question revived the conversation. They wanted to start their own business, doing something that reflected their true interests and abilities. After exploring possibilities ranging from a food truck to a ski camp, they struck their "Eureka!" idea: buying a local home care agency franchise.

The closer we looked at the idea, the more excited they became. Sandy was an excellent nurse, and Bob prided himself on his managerial and sales skills, so it checked those boxes. A franchise also made sense to them. They felt it would lower their business risks by providing a support network and marketing opportunities. This seemed less daunting than striking out entirely on their own.

With that discovery, we brought in a franchise coach who helped the Burkes narrow their search. After a review of a few different options, they landed on the health care industry—in particular, care for the sick and/or elderly in their homes.

If you are not familiar with home health care, it's interesting to note there are two major types. A **home care agency** provides in-home non-medical services, including bathing, driving, laundry, meal preparation, and companionship. A **home health agency** provides in-home medical care, such as nursing and therapy. As a registered nurse, Sandy knew she did not want to be in the business of delivering medical care, because of the additional liabilities and certifications involved. From a business perspective, Bob also preferred home care vs. home health, so they could seek private payments instead of having to deal with collecting on insurance claims.

Bottom line, their business plans were in place. Now, back to the financials. Where was the start-up money going to come from?

THE BIRTH OF A HOME CARE BUSINESS

If you've ever thought about shifting careers midlife, you probably already know there's a lot to plan for beyond the obvious.

Along with finding the right franchise to buy into, we would need to figure out how Bob was going to leave his company and maximize his benefits. How would removing a steady income, dependable benefits, and consistent annual savings impact their retirement goals? Were Bob and Sandy prepared to work longer than they may have originally planned, and save more aggressively along the way? What other lifestyle trade-offs might be required? For example, they had been considering sending Elizabeth to a private high school for more individualized attention, but of course that came with a cost.

In short, we had to throw away their old financial plan and create a new one.

Fortunately, the prospect of removing the corporate handcuffs was a strong motivator. At one point in our ongoing conversations, Bob stopped mid-sentence, and exclaimed, "Wow, I haven't been this excited about working for years!" Sandy laughed in agreement.

Still, we had to figure out how to pay for it. Start-up costs totaled around $350,000, with $70,000 due within 14 days of signing the contract. These costs included:

- Franchise fee: $250,000 including a $70,000 deposit.
- Rental space: $3,000 per month ($36,000 to plan for a year in advance).

- Other costs: $65,000 paid to the franchisor for a marketing and social media blitz.

On the flip side, the Burkes had $40,000 in liquid cash; if they tapped their tax-deferred retirement accounts for the rest, we estimated federal and state taxes and early withdrawal penalties totaling around $135,000. That would be on top of the $350,000. Not to mention their own living expenses.

Clearly, this was a distressing challenge. We explored a number of possible solutions, such as spreading the taxable distributions over two years, borrowing against their retirement accounts or home equity, taking the cash value out of their life insurance, or spending money earmarked for the kids' college. None of these ideas seemed sufficient or satisfactory.

Fortunately, all was not lost. Their franchise coach, Beth Anne, next brought up the idea of a ROBS plan.

WHAT'S A ROBS PLAN?

A ROBS, or Rollover for Business Startup plan, is an ERISA retirement plan (similar to a Profit-Sharing 401(k) plan) that allows you to use tax-deferred retirement monies to fund a new business. The ROBS plan would own the company, structured as a C corporation. The Burkes could move retirement monies into it, and as long as the money was used to pay for business expenses (such as operating expenses, wages, etc.), it would remain a tax-deferred asset. That would mean any money spent would be kept in the business, with no $135,000 in taxable distributions and penalties!

Still, I hesitated. As great as that sounded to the Burkes, there were a couple of challenging components to consider. First, there would be extra layers of complexity to registering the business as a C corporation. A pass-through entity, such as an LLC or S corporation, was more common.

Also, and most importantly, a ROBS plan can have a disastrous impact on any well-laid financial plan. By moving your assets to a ROBS plan, you are taking large amounts of money out of what should be your well-diversified investment portfolio and buying an individual security—your business—which is now a significant, highly concentrated position in your total wealth.

I generally recommend investing no more than 10% of your assets in any one position. In this case, **over 90%** of the Burkes' investable assets would be held in one concentrated position. Like Enron employees who had lost everything after investing most of their 401(k) in their company's stock in the early 2000s, the Burkes would lose almost everything if their business failed. There would be no getting the money back.

The Burkes and I discussed this critical point at length. Did they want to take on that much risk? Eyes wide open, they said yes, and committed to the plan.

THE BURKES ARE DEALT A FORTUITOUS CURVE BALL

As they were preparing for Bob to leave his company, Metalworks gave Bob his walking papers. While being laid off would normally be bad news, the timing actually worked out to his benefit. It provided six months of severance pay, so he could continue to draw an income while he and Sandy worked on their new business full-time.

The downsizing also added to their confidence that they had made the correct decision for their future. They rolled forward with the ROBS plan, naming their company Elias Family Holdings—a combination of their children's names, Elizabeth and Nicholas.

NEW CHAPTER

As soon as Bob signed the severance papers, he and Sandy jumped on a plane to California with the signed franchise agreement, ready to start a new chapter. When I met with the Burkes after they returned, they told me that they could have flown there on the wings of their own excitement. They had butterflies thinking about the next steps of their journey, but were beyond excited to get started. I was nearly as excited for them.

Fast forward to 2021, and the Burkes just received a $1.2 million valuation on their business and have recently closed on a new territory in Vermont. As I mentioned at the outset, they are now considering whether they might sell the company in a couple of years to fund their dream retirement: purchasing a boat, traveling up and down the East Coast, and transitioning to a life without work.

With good planning and a complete understanding of the risks, this family was ready to take on the challenges (and believe me, there were many) of starting their own business. Even had events not turned out as well as they did, I'd like to think it was the right decision for the Burkes when they chose to hit that big red RESET button. They took charge of their financial future and demanded change. Not only are they content with the results, they were able to pass on valuable life lessons to their children, including ones of determination and grit in the face of setbacks.

Dreams don't always come easy, if at all. But the sense of accomplishment we can achieve by realizing them is often worth the risks involved.

What are your dreams?

IN SUMMARY

- With good financial advice and careful planning, there are routes out of and between careers that still preserve financial stability.

THE POWER
TO PLAY

WHEN SHOULD YOU START TAKING SOCIAL SECURITY BENEFITS?

Marguerita Cheng, CFP®, RICP®

Marguerita Cheng educates the public, policy makers, and media about the benefits of competent, ethical financial planning. As a CERTIFIED FINANCIAL PLANNER™ professional and founder of financial advisory firm Blue Ocean Global Wealth, she helps her clients meet their life goals through the proper management of financial resources. She is passionate about helping them navigate some of life's most difficult issues—divorce, death, career changes, caring for aging relatives—so they can feel confident and in control of their finances. Rita is a regular columnist for Kiplinger and MarketWatch, and a past spokesperson for the AARP Financial Freedom Campaign. Marguerita volunteers her time as a SoleMate, or charity runner, for Girls on the Run, raising money for scholarships for girls to lead healthy, active & confident lives.

A FTER NEARLY 20 years of financial planning and helping clients achieve goals, I have learned that personal finance is personal. And nowhere is that more relevant than in the question of when to begin social security benefits.

Of course, the "one size fits all" example that we have all heard is "wait until you reach full retirement age," but I am grateful to have had the privilege to work with clients facing unique life circumstances who chose different strategies that delivered so much more value to them than the "wait until you reach full retirement age" strategy ever would have.

A CANCER SURVIVOR'S DECISION
TO TAKE BENEFITS EARLY

In 2000, Leonard was 59 and experiencing many life transitions. He was a two-time cancer survivor, so had always thought he would predecease his wife. But sadly she suffered two mini-strokes, then had a major stroke which she did not survive.

At the same time, the company he worked for offered him early retirement with a generous 18-month severance package and health care for life. The severance funds he was awarded would take him to age 61.

Leonard knew that social security benefits could begin at 62 but was worried about what he would do for income between the ages of 61 and 62.

In general, I advise my clients to keep six to 12 months of cash reserves (for retirees, I recommend at least 12–24 months). Candidly, he had closer to six months' worth, but his annual leave/sick leave and incentive pay brought him up to 12 months, which coincided with his 62nd birthday. At this point, his kids were grown and financially independent.

Living alone, newly retired, with an understanding of the likelihood of cancer recurrence, Leonard decided—after taking my advice—that it would bring greater value to his life to begin receiving social security benefits as early as possible (age 62). It is true that the monthly monetary amount was lower than it would have been had he waited until full retirement age, but the immediate modest cash flow (plus his pension) brought him security and comfort in the new realities he faced.

He eventually remarried, to Martha, whom he was introduced to by his daughter. Martha happened to be collecting a Civil Service Retirement System pension that made her ineligible for social security survivor benefits. With Leonard accepting the benefits that were available to him, they were able to travel to Europe, enjoy each other's company, work on home improvement projects, and have the peace of mind that comes with having a sustainable source of retirement income.

When Leonard was 64, cancer unfortunately struck again, and this time it spread to his liver. He passed away just before his 66th birthday. I will always remember this because I always visited Leonard and Martha after the Christmas holiday each year.

I attended his memorial service, and Martha told me, "I am thankful for the amazing years we had together. I am going to miss him so much, but I am thankful for the incredible memories. We visited Europe twice together before he became too ill to travel."

In Leonard's unique story, the decision to begin accepting benefits at age 62 made a huge difference in enjoying his last years of life. Considering Martha's pension from the Civil Service Retirement System and his adult children's self-sufficiency, Leonard truly made a decision that had no downsides—even from the perspective of survivor benefits.

Understanding and weighing the factors of health history, marital status, whether children are still financially dependent, and early retirement package elements are all important considerations— even when "wait until you reach full retirement age" dominates the conversation.

DECIDING TO WAIT
UNTIL AGE 70

Paul was a Chinese immigrant who arrived in America with a degree in applied mathematics from a Taiwanese university. In the 1960s he fled communism and sought a better life in the United States.

A lifelong learner and hard worker, Paul joined Toastmasters International to improve his public speaking, communication, and leadership skills. While Paul was new to the world of capitalism and wealth building, his proficiency in mathematics made him a great financial planner, especially with guidance from professional advisors.

In 1992, when Paul retired from a large technology company at the age of 60 to begin his consulting business, his wife, Eileen, was only 46 and working part-time. Social Security regulations have changed some in the last 30 years, but, just like today, Paul could have started receiving Social Security benefits at age 62.

But Paul and Eileen had the courage to question this option. Even in the 1990s, there were many experts advising 62-year-olds to take their social security benefits as soon as possible.

At this point in their lives, they had kids who were teenagers and in their 20s, and Paul was receiving a pension from his former employer that covered the family's core expenses. Their mortgage was not quite paid off, but Paul's pension comfortably covered this expense for the remaining payments.

While many people in Paul's position could have stayed at the large tech firm, Paul had always been interested in joining a consulting firm and working with smaller companies to help them solve problems and grow.

This unique situation could have inspired a lot of Social Security benefit strategies. They asked themselves, "Should we start receiving benefits at age 62 to pad the household income while Eileen continues to work?" and "Should we delay until Paul reaches full retirement age—or even 70—to increase the monthly amount?"

With income from three sources (the pension, the consulting business, and Eileen's employment), I wanted to help Paul and Eileen see that waiting until Paul's 70th year to allow the benefits to reach the maximum amount might be the best option. After seeing the income streams and projecting earning potential and expenses over the next several years, Paul and Eileen decided to delay receiving Paul's Social Security benefits until age 70.

But other research factored into this decision: Paul and Eileen learned that when spouses are both retired, two Social Security checks arrive each month. When one spouse dies, the check with the lower amount stops coming in regardless of who was originally entitled to the benefits. In Paul and Eileen's case, the Social Security benefit to which he was entitled was much larger than the one earned by Eileen.

Paul realized that by deferring his benefit to age 70, he would lock in a larger benefit. He knew that most likely he would predecease Eileen, so by waiting until age 70, he was providing the largest benefit possible for her through spousal benefits.

In the years between his retirement at age 60 and the beginning of social security benefits at age 70, Paul's consulting business provided a steady income and a sense of meaning in his life.

In fact, Paul said he felt so fortunate to be doing the work he loved that at times he could not believe companies run by younger people would hire him as a technology consultant.

The incomes they received from the pension, the consulting business, and Eileen's work ensured that their life was comfortable and fulfilling. Sadly, Paul passed away due to Parkinson's Disease at age 82, leaving Eileen widowed at age 68.

Social Security is the foundation of a retirement income strategy. The benefits provide security, and they receive preferential tax treatment. The rules about claiming Social Security have changed over the last several decades, but the rules for survivors (widows and widowers) have not. There are still major opportunities to help individuals when they are most vulnerable.

While many say, "It pays to wait," it is stories like those of Leonard and Paul and Eileen that make me say, "It pays to educate!" My deep belief about Social Security benefits is that you can live your best retirement if you take time to work with a professional financial planner to educate yourself about the details of Social Security benefits.

IN SUMMARY

- When considering when to claim Social Security, every individual's situation is different.
- For some people, with the right planning and financial advice, claiming as early as possible makes the most sense. For others, deferring claims makes more sense.

SUCCESSFUL TRANSFER OF THE FAMILY BUSINESS

Brett K. Fellows, CFP®

Brett Fellows, CFP® began his career in the golf industry in 1996. Eventually, he worked his way up to vice president of a multi-facility golf operating company. In 2005, Brett decided to take what he had learned as a small business owner to help other entrepreneurs with business and financial planning. As a result, he founded Oak Capital Advisors and has since dedicated his career to helping business owners reduce risk, minimize taxes, and invest smarter so they can confidently retire on their own terms.

Brett is a CERTIFIED FINANCIAL PLANNER™ professional and a proud graduate of Bentley University, a national leader in business education.

"I'M GLAD YOU could both make it today," I said, shaking hands with Mark and Ann. "It's important that we get this right."

Mark sat down across from me and crossed his arms. He was average height, in his early 60s, and had a receding hairline and dark circles under his eyes. His wife, Ann, sat down next to him. She was in her late 50s and tall, with short dark hair that was graying at the temples.

Mark and Ann owned a small yet profitable commercial moving company. They bought the business from the previous owner almost 30 years ago, when Mark was one of two full-time employees. At that time, the moving company was more of a local mom-and-pop shop that served businesses in the Charleston area. Today, Mark and Ann's moving company serves the Carolinas, Georgia, and eastern Tennessee. Last year, the business generated over $3m dollars in revenue.

Mark began, "As I mentioned when we spoke on the phone, it's taken me a long time to build my moving business. But lately Ann and I have been talking about retirement and how nice it would be to spend more time with our grandchildren. We've been doing this for 30 years and want to pass the torch to our son Paul. He's been active in the family business for years, overseeing the books and payroll. He knows the business inside and out, and I'm confident that he's ready to replace me. However, he's 30 years old and still paying off student loans from college. He doesn't have the cash saved to buy me out, so Ann and I want to gift him a controlling share of the business.

The thing is, we have two other children: Mary and John. Neither wants any part of the moving business, and we've always supported that decision. But we also want to keep things fair, financially. We're not sure how to do that, though, without triggering a huge tax bill. We also don't want to upset anyone."

Ann spoke up next. "Of course, we want what's best for our children. But we also want to make sure we can still retire comfortably if we do this. We've always been careful with our money, and both Mark and I have been contributing to our retirement accounts for decades. However, we've never sat down with a financial planner to see how much we actually need to have saved for retirement. We just don't want to jump the gun or make any big mistakes."

KEEPING UNCLE SAM AT BAY

"I understand your concerns," I said. "Don't worry, you're not the first family to confront these challenges. The good news is you're already doing better than most business owners since you have a succession plan in place. Let's start there. Do you have any idea what your business is worth currently?"

"Well," Mark said, "That's another thing. This may be strange to say, but the business is doing really well, which adds to our uncertainty. Our projections show cash flow growing by at least 15% year over year for the next three years. I'm assuming this growth will make it even more difficult to transfer the business to Paul—at least when considering the tax impact. Ann and I don't want to leave money on the table, either. At the end of the day, maintaining family harmony is most important to us, but we want to be smart about it. We don't want the IRS to be the primary beneficiary of our hard-earned money."

"Got it," I said, noting Mark's concerns. "Given your interest in transferring the business, let's set up a follow-up meeting to look at a few scenarios. Then, we can start to develop your retirement plan and identify the right gifting strategies for Mary and John. Sound good?"

Mark and Ann nodded and relaxed back in their seats. We pulled up our calendars and scheduled our next meeting.

PLANNING FOR A
SECURE RETIREMENT

Over the next three months, Mark, Ann, and I organized an in-depth review of their company's business structure and financials. We enlisted the help of an attorney with small business expertise, as well as a business valuation specialist in the commercial moving industry. Our first objective was to determine a fair value for the business to get a better idea of the potential tax implications.

Once we had that number, we could design an efficient wealth transfer strategy. As Mark said in our first meeting, he didn't want the IRS to be the largest beneficiary of the family's hard-earned money. With help from Mark and Ann's accountant and estate planning attorney, we developed a strategy leveraging trusts and a family limited liability company (LLC) to transfer a controlling share of the business to Paul and equal cash amounts to Mary and John while minimizing Uncle Sam's portion.

With that behind us, we still needed to address Mark and Ann's retirement plan. They had become accustomed to a certain lifestyle while working, and they didn't want that to change once they stopped. In fact, they expected to increase their travel expenses during retirement, since Mary and John lived in Chicago and Denver, respectively.

We combined their estimated payout from the sale of the business with their personal retirement savings. Then, we developed a retirement income and investment strategy that allowed them to enjoy a comfortable standard of living after stepping away from the family business. After looking at a handful of different scenarios, Mark and Ann seemed more confident in their decision to retire.

TELLING THE CHILDREN

With a strategy in place, Mark and Ann indicated that they were ready to tell the rest of the family about their decision. "We're excited to tell the children," Mark told me at the end of our meeting that day. "We don't know how they're going to react, though. What do we say if they push back?"

"Why don't you suggest they meet you here, on neutral territory?" I said. "That way I can help facilitate the conversation and step in if tensions start to run high."

Mark and Ann agreed that it would probably be best to have a third party present. Two weeks later, I met with Mark, Ann, Paul, Mary, and John to help facilitate an open dialogue between parents and children. Despite the family's closeness, Mark and Ann had never discussed the family finances with their children before. Though civil, the conversation was fueled by emotion.

Mary and John shared their honest opinions about the family business for the first time. Although they supported Paul taking over from their father, they had concerns about what that meant for them and their financial futures.

DEVELOPING A FAMILY LEGACY

The family also discussed what they wanted their legacy to be beyond the family business. Mark and Ann communicated their desire to direct part of the family's wealth towards philanthropic causes. Ann had lost a brother to childhood leukaemia, and she steadfastly donates to St. Jude every year.

This prompted Mary and John to express an interest in creating a family foundation. They even said they'd like to run it one day if given the opportunity. Mary was passionate about protecting the environment, while John spent a lot of time volunteering for a crisis hotline. While they had no interest in the family business, they very much wanted to be part of the family's legacy of charitable giving.

Once the initial tension subsided, Mark, Ann, and I explained the strategies we had developed to transfer the business to Paul and equal parts of the family wealth to Mary and John. All three children seemed satisfied with the plan, and the conversation turned to Mark and Ann's retirement. The children agreed that retiring was the right decision, and that they were glad their parents were taking more time for themselves.

Our next directive was to sit down together and develop a charitable giving strategy. Mark, Ann, and I scheduled a follow-up meeting, and Mary and John said they'd be interested in calling in so they could share their ideas. Meanwhile, Mark and Ann successfully transitioned the business to Paul, who has since managed to exceed Mark's growth projections and pay off his student loans.

Today, Mark and Ann are comfortably retired. With the sale of the business behind them and their most pressing financial objectives met, they now enjoy traveling, volunteer work, and spending more time with their children and grandchildren.

IN SUMMARY

- Start with a succession plan and some sound financial advice.
- Your financial planner can be with you every step of the way, from deciding whether and when to retire, to sitting down with the children to discuss the financial implications.

THE POWER TO CHANGE

CENTS DON'T ALWAYS MAKE SENSE

Matt Fizell, CFP®

Matt Fizell is the owner of Harmony Wealth, a fee-only Investment Advisory firm located in the Madison, WI area. Matt founded Harmony Wealth for healthcare professionals and small business owners to find the harmony of the "how" and "why" of their financial resources. He was named as one of Investopedia.com's Top 100 Most Influential Financial Advisors in the United States in 2020, and also serves the Financial Planning Association's Next Generation through the "You're a Financial Planner, Now What?" podcast, which has amassed over 500,000 downloads. He has also been featured by prominent publications such as *Forbes*, CNBC, and Consumer Reports.

In addition to working in his financial planning practice, Matt serves his community through financial literacy efforts with the local Foster Care Unit serving the broader Dane County area. He also provides volunteering efforts through "Wake the World", a 501(c)(3) non-profit organization that shares the joy of watersports such as skiing and wakeboarding with those in foster communities.

What started out as a quick meeting to help Katie get started on paying off her student debt quickly turned into a conversation of fear, and of tears.

Although we were meeting over Zoom on this occasion, the emotions coming through Katie's webcam were cutting straight through me.

Katie was a single mother of four children, and had been widowed only a few years prior. While my mother is not widowed, she too raised me on her own, and the flood of anxiety Katie was experiencing was too familiar to me.

Additionally, Katie was going through the process of ending a relationship with someone whom she had purchased a home and moved in with, while also being six months away from obtaining her MBA.

You could hear the level of exhaustion, and even a degree of hopelessness, in her voice as she began to run the numbers in her head.

Today's meeting had been scheduled as a brief follow-up to a meeting which had occurred two weeks ago.

WHEN YOU KNOW, YOU KNOW

Right as we began the Zoom meeting, I could tell something was bothering Katie. Many of us have been in those situations before, where we can simply hear the trouble in someone's voice or see it in their face.

Katie did not have the energy she normally brings to the meeting. The normal sense of optimism in her voice was replaced by tension and anxiety. She was nervous about making a mistake in setting up her payments, or not paying them off in the best way possible.

From a tactical standpoint, this gave us the decision between making a lump-sum payment, or paying them off steadily over time. In this case, the tactics were less important, because we had already determined that she would be fine either way.

Knowing this, however, did not make the decision any less stressful for Katie.

To add to this fear, Katie was not particularly comfortable using the online payment portal of her student loan processor, and one objective of the meeting was simply to walk her through this and get the payments set up.

I asked Katie if everything was okay, or if there were any points from the previous meeting we should cover first before we got started in logging into her student loan account together.

"I'm fine," she replied. "It's a busy point in the semester and I'm getting the kids ready for school too."

Those were both incredibly real and valid points as to why Katie sounded the way she did. Every minute of Katie's day was valuable to her, and we proceeded to get started.

I should have listened to my initial gut reaction. There was more to the story, and I distinctly remember feeling there was something deeper happening inside of Katie's mind. Katie was not usually the kind of person to hold back what she was feeling though, and holding on to that fact allowed me to move forward with the meeting without thinking twice.

EASY DOESN'T MEAN SIMPLE

This particular meeting on my calendar didn't have too much for me to prepare. How hard could it possibly be to log in to an account and set up a payment?

We logged in, and saw what we already knew. Regardless of what we chose, it was well within Katie's ability to pay off the debt.

I distinctly remember, "Well, this was a lot easier than I thought it would be," running through my head as we saw the numbers flash up on the screen.

But then, something completely unexpected happened.

Katie broke out in tears and said sadly, "How on earth am I going to pay this off?"

I was completely caught off guard, and frankly, I was stunned. I did not know what to say next.

Katie began listing off the other obligations she was worried about. College savings, clothes, and food for her growing children. No longer having half of the mortgage paid by her significant other. Another semester's worth of bills and tuition for her MBA.

We knew all the pieces of Katie's financial puzzle. We had carefully modeled out the variables and knew within a degree of certainty Katie would be okay. "We just talked about this," I thought to myself.

What I quickly began to realize is this was not about the long-term success. Instead, it was about today, next week, next month, and next year.

The emotions Katie was feeling in that moment could not be solved with an intricate spreadsheet, some fancy graphics showing the details of her cash flow, or a probability of success. She needed to see the financial planning process improving her financial situation step by step.

This is something many of us as financial advisors commonly forget to consider. Logical models don't consider the emotional part of our financial lives, the pain we and our clients sometimes feel when we can't see through the fog of our busy and complicated financial lives.

Life isn't a bunch of neat numbers on a spreadsheet; it is messy.

THE REAL PROBLEM

As I had felt in my stomach earlier, there was more to address in this meeting than what had initially been planned for.

Katie was drowning in the complexity of her current life situation, and who could blame her?

The problem for Katie was less about having enough financial resources, but instead about having time and clarity to understand where her ship was heading as it sailed across a foggy sea of restless water.

Information anyone could possibly want on this field is a few clicks away on the internet. Simply regurgitating information isn't what this, or any meeting with a financial planner, is really about.

As financial planners, what we actually do is help others make sense of their dollars and cents. That's it.

Katie knew that on paper she was going to be fine. What she didn't know, was how to make sense of how it was actually going to work over the next couple of years when it came to other areas of her life.

This isn't easy to do when a bunch of numbers go into a black box that is the financial calculator, which then tells you that you will be "okay" 10 years from now.

Katie didn't have time to sit down and work through each item line by line and figure out how the reports we created came to be. As we sat there and talked through what her average day looks like, I drew back on the experiences of my childhood, and how few conversations we had about money while I was growing up.

Much like my mom, Katie's time was completely consumed with raising her children, maintaining a household, and trying to improve her career by furthering her education.

In the increasingly busy world we find ourselves living in, there simply isn't enough time in the day to do each task required to go through life, especially with how fast our world can change.

Katie's situation needed to be made as plain and simple as possible, and that is what we set out to do next.

SEEING THROUGH THE FOG

Considering how crazy Katie's life is, her ability to remain organized is nothing short of heroic.

She is still to this day one of the best budgeters I have ever seen, sticking to it nearly to perfection on a monthly basis while living in the beautiful but expensive Pacific Northwest.

Knowing this about Katie, I knew showing her how she spent her money would be something she could ground herself with when facing the uncertainty of her near-term ability to care for her children.

The budget would provide the step by step information we needed to cut through the fog.

As we looked through her budget, she said, "There is absolutely nothing in here that I regret spending money on, but there are a few things I could probably cut out if push came to shove."

When she arrived at what the current total amount would be, and what her current savings balance was, we had a simple division math problem to complete to see how long she could go without touching any of her long-term savings.

Our simple calculation determined it would be 12 months if she made the monthly payment on her loans, and 10 months if she paid off the entire balance today.

"What should I do?" Katie asked.

We had arrived at the same question we finished the previous meeting on, and the answer was still the same as last time. It did not matter. There were always other accounts we *could* pull from or expenses Katie had identified she *could* cut from her budget, if she was not able to complete her degree on time.

The problem with "should" and "could" is that it generally means there will be more than one option to consider the pros and cons behind. This is where Katie's fog was clouding her decision-making abilities.

"What do you feel would make you the most comfortable?" I replied.

You could see the tension wash away from Katie's face, and she brushed away the trails left behind from her tears with the cuff of her sweater.

"Well, I do not want to find myself cutting back on anything, especially when it comes to caring for my kids and saving for their college, that is important to me," she said.

Before I could reply, she cut in with, "But if I only make the monthly payments, I'd be paying interest, and that is something we should avoid, right?"

We had quickly jumped back into the pros and cons. It is an incredibly tough aspect of working through financial decisions, where math can almost always show us a "better" answer.

The fog these better answers can create is one of the most difficult parts of personal finance, especially for someone like Katie who already has a million different moving pieces in her mind.

"What if instead of thinking of the interest as a penalty, we thought of it as a small amount of money you are paying to make sure you can do what you want to do for your kids?" I asked.

The smile came back to Katie's face. She had not seen or thought about it that way before, and in this instance, taking that approach did not make much of a difference in the long run.

I am sure at this point you can easily guess which option Katie chose.

We set up the monthly payment to get started, logged out, and began to wrap up the meeting.

"Why could I not see that 30 minutes ago?" she said. "Thank you for being so patient with me today, for something so stupid."

I reassured her the problem was not stupid, it is how life works sometimes. Fog can get in the way and make it hard to see where we are going, which is uncomfortable for most people.

For Katie, living the best on-paper financial life was not going to allow her to live *her best life*. Being fully optimized for what makes sense to her did not make the most sense when it came to the dollars and cents. But that's okay—the best life has to be what works for each individual.

Katie came to the meeting looking for someone to come up with a solution to what she was feeling that day.

And you know who came up with the solution during that meeting?

Katie did. What she needed was someone to help connect the dots on the map on her way to the destination.

IN SUMMARY

- Finances can look simple on a spreadsheet, but seem much more challenging in the context of busy, messy life.
- A good financial advisor helps clients cut through the fog of other concerns to identify the best financial routes forward.
- Living the best on-paper financial life might not allow you to live *your best life.*

WHERE WE BELONG

Kevin D. Christensen, CFP®

Kevin is a founder and LPL financial planner at Aligned Financial Planning, focused on helping charitably inclined individuals, business owners, and donors of non-profits align their money with their personal values.

Kevin is involved with Big Brothers Big Sisters of San Diego County as a board member, mentor, and speaker. Additionally, he provides pro bono planning to the less fortunate through the San Diego Financial Literacy Center. With a degree in business finance from Point Loma Nazarene University (PLNU), Kevin continues to remain involved with his alma mater as a board member of the PLNU Business Alumni Association. He holds advanced designations as a CERTIFIED FINANCIAL PLANNER™ practitioner and Accredited Investment Fiduciary®. When Kevin isn't working or involved with charities, you'll find him exploring new restaurants, playing golf or spending time outdoors. Kevin, his wife, Alyc, and their two children, live in San Diego and love spending time in their neighborhood.

Kevin Christensen is a registered representative with, and offers securities and advisory services through, LPL Financial, a registered investment advisor. Member FINRA/SIPC.

Where do retired naval officer Daniel and his wife Rae call home?

Is it the house they've owned for 42 years in a small San Diego beach town, even though they've only lived in it for part of that time? Or perhaps it's one of the many government quarters Daniel was stationed in over the years in Hawaii, or Japan, or Monterey, CA, at which Rae—who was a teacher—and the kids would frequently join him.

Maybe home is the Oregon family farm Daniel grew up on—the one his great grandparents established in 1852, when they crossed the Rockies, the Great Plains, and the Cascades by wagon train. It's still in the family, and they still love to visit there from time to time.

Home might even be the nearby garage where they keep their 1963 Porsche, which Daniel bought new in 1962 while stationed on an aircraft carrier in Hong Kong. With more than 250,000 miles to its name, that bright red Porsche has traveled with them ever since, serving as the family car around the globe. She still revs up just fine.

One place Daniel and Rae are *not* yet ready to call home is the beautiful San Diego retirement community they now reside in, after many years of fruitful adventures. Daniel sums up his feelings about retirement living as follows: "It will probably never be home, as such, but it's where we belong."

PICKING THE RIGHT PLACE

Don't get me wrong. A few years after their move, I asked Daniel and Rae if they regretted the decision. They quickly confirmed they did not. There are many things they love about their new location and lifestyle. Many of their fellow military friends and other acquaintances live there as well, which is one reason they chose the place. Even during the Covid-19 pandemic, they weren't as isolated as they may otherwise have been. Rae is especially fond of hosting social gatherings, and looks forward to doing more of that soon.

Another plus: They chose a community relatively close to their former home, so there was no need to find new stores, change doctors, or otherwise recreate those kinds of connections.

What about their San Diego beach community house, which they'd decided to sell during the transition? Their son had been against the idea; their daughter had been all for it. Daniel had gone in with mixed feelings, while Rae had felt it was time. In hindsight, they both agreed it was a good idea. "Here, if anything breaks, they just fix it," says Rae.

Most of all, they are relieved to be where they won't need to place heavy demands on their children should their health decline. They remain in close contact with their son and daughter, who have relocated to the East Coast, and near Portland, Oregon, respectively. Daniel and Rae are glad their kids were able to make these moves without having to worry about what might happen to Mom and Dad.

In fact, health concerns were largely the driving force behind their decision to become retirement community residents. To be accepted into the community they preferred, neither could be diagnosed with dementia or Parkinson's disease at the outset. And while neither had been, Daniel had been exhibiting some Parkinson's symptoms. For better or worse, they felt the decision had become a "now or never" choice.

So, after what felt like an overly rushed sale of the family home, the move was made.

GRAY CLOUDS AND SILVER LININGS

Even under ideal conditions, major life transitions are rarely easy—even for a military man and his wife, long used to frequent changes of address. As often as they moved around, they always knew they owned a home, to which they could return. It bothered Daniel more than he thought it would to no longer have that sense of place, where they got to call all the shots. And they both miss the days when Rae could relax with her gardening while Daniel would tinker in his workshop.

It also took an emotional toll on them when they had to downsize from their five-bedroom home (where they'd stashed all their stuff over the years), to a tidy two-bedroom apartment. As it turned out, they ended up having to make the move on a relatively tight timeline. This was stressful and traumatic. Rae describes having to hurriedly get rid of a number of childhood keepsakes she wished she had kept. "I hadn't looked at most of them for years, but I miss knowing I still have them," she sighs.

On the other hand, with their less encumbered lifestyle, they also hope to travel again soon, beyond just road trips to visit their daughter. South Africa has long been on the bucket list as one of the regions they have never been to. And Daniel has been studying Spanish, with an itch to get to use it abroad.

FIGURING OUT THE FINANCIALS

While Daniel and Rae are not suffering financially, neither did they want to waste money as they transitioned to their new lifestyle. This is another major milestone challenge families face, and happily one I was able to assist them with as their financial advisor.

There were certainly many angles to consider.

First, could they afford to make the move in general, including a substantial buy-in, as well as ongoing monthly payments? After looking over their pensions and other assets, we agreed the answer was "yes."

But, there was that house. Not only had it created decades of memories for them, it had built up considerable resale value, which would translate into a *seven-figure* capital gains tax upon sale.

Yes, you read that correctly. They would owe taxes of over $1m.

This took some planning. Even with the $500,000 capital gain exclusion when a couple sells their primary residence, that still left a lot of taxable income on the table.

Fortunately, we came up with a three-pronged defense that included generating some deductible expenses, incurring capital losses in their investment portfolio, and—most significantly—fulfilling their charitable intent, which had long been important to them anyway.

COMING OUT AHEAD THROUGH CHARITABLE GIVING

Daniel and Rae are very charitably inclined, having supported countless causes throughout their lives. By helping them establish a donor advised fund (DAF) in the same year they incurred their home sale gains, we were able to prefund at least five years of their future charitable giving, while offsetting some of those gains. In fact, they liked their DAF so much, they decided to donate more appreciated stock a few years later.

It's money they'd likely have been donating to their favorite causes anyway, such as their church, the local hospital, and the San Diego Zoo (where their grandchildren have personalized paver stones to visit). By being deliberate about the timing of their DAF donations, especially since they can't itemize their deductions any longer after selling their home, Daniel and Rae have been able to minimize many taxable gains they'd otherwise have incurred. Even better, they've named their daughter as the successor to the DAF, and she is very excited about this valuable gift being a part of her inheritance.

APARTMENT, SWEET APARTMENT

Shortly after Daniel and Rae moved into their retirement community—before Covid-19 had hit—they invited me and my wife over for dinner. It was meaningful to see them enjoying their new place, although I remember Daniel saying he felt more like he was vacationing in a nice timeshare than settling into a new home.

Maybe as they make new memories over time, that feeling will shift. Maybe not. Either way, I hope they make it to South Africa and back sometime soon. If they could resume some of their wider travels, perhaps their new digs will start to feel like a place to call home every time they return.

IN SUMMARY

- Charitable giving can be a way to express your values, leave a legacy, and ease the burden of taxes.

———————

FINDING A NEW LIFE PLAN

Michael H. Baker, CFP®, CIMA®, RICP®, RMA®

Michael H. Baker is a manager and founding member at Vertex Capital Advisors LLC, a financial services firm that specializes in financial planning and retirement income strategies. Michael is passionate about showing clients they have no reason to fear money, finances and the "financial guys." He knows many people view financial planning as a tedious process, something that they simply must endure. His goal is to change that.

Michael is a member of the Financial Planning Association (FPA®), the Investment Management Consultants Association® (IMCA®), the Advisor Growth Community (the AGC®), and Kingdom Advisors® (a community of Christian Financial Advisors).

Investment advisory and financial planning services offered through Advisory Alpha, LLC, a SEC Registered Investment Advisor. Insurance, consulting and education services offered through Vertex Capital Advisors. Vertex Capital Advisors is a separate and unaffiliated entity from Advisory Alpha, LLC.

IT'S EXTREMELY RARE for clients to call me after business hours. Usually, they will send a brief email asking if we can hop on a call the next day. Thus, it was very odd when Sally rang me one evening around 7.30 pm.

I can still vividly remember her call because of what happened next. I was rocking my newborn son in his glider, trying to get him to go to sleep, when I answered and heard Sally's frantic voice.

"Michael?"

"Hi Sally, are you okay?"

"Michael, John is dead."

Time froze for a few seconds. I didn't know what to do. For a moment, I had a mental flash that forced me to clarify what I'd just heard.

"What? Can you tell me that again?"

To the best of her ability, Sally began to explain that the coroner was standing in her living room. She and a sheriff's deputy had come over to inform her that John had suffered a massive heart attack at a friend's house. He was gone.

Sally lived only a few minutes from me, and something in me said I needed to go over there. I didn't know what else to do. I quickly briefed my wife on the situation and asked her to take over my bedtime duties.

When I arrived at Sally's house, she was sitting on her couch in tears. She looked at me and apologized for calling.

"I know you've got a family to take care of," she said.

"But, I just didn't know what else to do."

The next few hours were one of the most emotional experiences I've ever had with a client. I sat with Sally, and we called each of her daughters one by one to break the news. Hearing each daughter learn that Daddy was no longer alive was a surreal experience. I'll never forget it.

The next morning, I called to check on Sally, and I learned that each of the girls had already driven into town to be with her. I went by a local Chick-Fil-A and grabbed some breakfast for them, delivering it to Sally's house on my way to the office.

As I visited with them, the questions were already beginning to materialize about Sally's financial future. I gave them all hugs and told them that they didn't need to worry.

Everything was going to be okay. I could handle the financial stuff. All they needed to do was take care of each other and grieve as a family.

It may sound insensitive to admit this next part, but part of financial planning is to consider unpleasant scenarios. Death can be an uncomfortable subject to cover, but the loss of a spouse is something that I feel should always be discussed when working with married couples. Our team had already prepared for this day.

Unfortunately, we were experiencing this loss way ahead of schedule. Knowing that we had planned for this possibility didn't numb the emotional pain Sally was feeling. However, our preparation allowed Sally to have an advantage that can be invaluable when experiencing a traumatic event—time.

A sudden jolt of this magnitude understandably creates a flood of emotions. It should come as no surprise that intense feelings and stress can short circuit our ability to make wise financial decisions. The fact that Sally wasn't going to be forced into making hasty financial decisions was a tremendous win.

BEGINNING AGAIN

A few weeks after John's funeral, Sally decided it was time to sit down and begin the transition process. Our team had already been working on some administrative tasks like account paperwork and insurance claims, but now it was time for Sally to take the reins. Sally assured us that she was ready.

In our firm, the planning process always requires the participation of both spouses. We make every effort to give each partner space to be heard and express their wants, concerns, and opinions about money.

Sally was always an active participant in those conversations; but she would often defer to John when it came to making the final decisions.

Sally would now be making decisions on her own. This new beginning put Sally in uncharted waters. I already knew that Sally was more than capable of directing her financial destiny; our team just needed to affirm her. Sally had raised three successful daughters, worked in financial services, and started a small business venture. She was just out of practice doing finances all by herself.

As you might expect, one of her greatest fears was whether or not she was going to be "okay" from an income standpoint. Financial security can be a vague concept, with many people using their feelings as a guide. Sally didn't want to be vague. She wanted to be clear and confident regarding any plan proposal we gave her for consideration.

The first thing we did together was walk Sally through the "old" planning blueprint. I asked her if she felt that the old plan reflected what she really wanted in her financial life. It didn't. So, I asked Sally for permission to start over and create a new blueprint, with her taking the lead.

NEW PRIORITIES

The results of these new planning discussions with Sally were not surprising. Even though our conversations tugged at emotions and yielded some tears, a new path for Sally began to emerge. Instead of a technical plan that was governed by stock selection and special tax provisions (the old plan), Sally had new priorities:

- Life was meant to be lived and enjoyed.
- Money wasn't meant to be hoarded.
- Income security was a top planning priority.
- Gifting to her daughters was a heartfelt desire.
- Relocating to be closer to her family was a priority for the whole family.

- A dream goal would be a second home in the mountains.

Using this new blueprint, we began working on Sally's objectives. Since cash flow is the backbone of any household economy, the first riddle Sally asked us to solve was how we would address her income needs.

We discovered that John, after one of our planning meetings, had signed up for a unique life insurance benefit at work that would pay his salary for six months if he passed away. Unlike traditional life insurance that pays a lump sum benefit, these funds were to be distributed as monthly payments. He'd never told Sally or our team that he'd done this, so it was a bittersweet surprise to learn that the normal household income would continue for a little while longer.

John's life insurance benefits provided Sally with much needed estate liquidity. She had enough income to continue paying her bills without any challenges, and she now had a large lump sum of tax-free dollars to use however she pleased. This nest egg would be crucial for Sally, as she had an interesting decision to make regarding her investments.

Prior to his death, John repositioned a large amount of company stock from his 401(k) plan that qualified for net unrealized appreciation (NUA) treatment. A full discussion of NUA stock is beyond the scope of this writing, but one unique feature of NUA stock is that it doesn't receive a step up in basis at death.

The original plan for John and Sally involved holding these shares for the dividend income, so the repositioning out of the 401(k) had made sense. Sally, however, was very nervous about having over half of her financial assets tied to one company. Being a more risk-averse investor than John, she wanted to know how she could diversify her portfolio and still generate income.

Diversification for Sally was possible, but it would come with a large tax bill. Selling the stock would trigger a large capital gains tax liability. Since no one likes taxes, Sally was conflicted about the best course of action.

I asked whether maintaining a concentrated position in one company would allow her to have peace of mind about her portfolio or be a source of anxiety.

Sally felt that she needed to invest in a way that allowed her to sleep at night. Due to the life insurance, she had the ability to cover the tax bill; so she decided to sell the large stock position and reinvest in a balanced portfolio. This new portfolio could still be used to generate income. Sally, however, felt more confident that her life savings were no longer tied to a single company's successes or failures.

As a final component of the income discussion, we re-evaluated Sally's social security income options. She was now eligible for two benefits—her worker benefit and the survivor's benefit. Since the survivor's benefit would grow if she chose to defer it, we proposed that she claim her worker benefit and maximize the survivor benefit by deferring until her full retirement age.

Many people can be tempted to go for the largest immediate benefit. Sally has longevity in her family, so she understood the need to think long term with her social security benefits. She decided to defer her larger benefit, choosing to maximize the payments over her lifetime.

As we concluded the income planning process for Sally, we determined that she would indeed have extra assets available to her if she wanted to do some gifting. As we talked through the impact that a financial gift would have for each of her girls, I asked, "What would have the greatest impact on them—a nice financial gift now or inheriting money years from now?"

All of Sally's daughters were in different phases of life. Sally and I discussed how neat it would be for Sally to experience the joy of gifting and witnessing how the funds were used. She had a unique opportunity to see the fruits of her gifts should she choose to move forward. Sally agreed, and we made arrangements for the gifts to be made.

LIFE AND PLANNING MOVE ON TOGETHER

One of the challenging aspects of personal financial planning is how unique each client engagement can be. Complexity can arise quickly when you consider that every client has different values, preferences, and subconscious money scripts that color their financial decision-making. This is why a good financial planning *process* can be invaluable to clients as they work toward their financial goals.

Sally has had many other life transitions in the few years since John's death. Securing her income needs for living expenses and life experiences was just the first step. Within the year, Sally moved out of state and became a caregiver to her mother, who passed away almost a year after John.

Sally has had the joy of becoming a grandmother three times over. She started another business venture at the age of 63, and we are still working on that mountain house. Life continues to move forward.

Through each of these transitions, we have had additional planning conversations to make sure that her money aligns with her values. From time to time, we still revisit the night that John passed away. It can still be emotional.

I'm thankful that Sally and John had started the planning process together. Through those early conversations, we laid the foundations for Sally's financial future to be protected. The planning process allowed Sally to rediscover her inner strength and empowered her to take control of her financial future. I can't think of a better testament to the power of financial planning than that.

IN SUMMARY

- A good financial plan and a committed advisor can help you weather the worst that life can throw at you.
- Through each of these transitions, we have additional planning conversations to make sure that a client's money aligns with their values.

———————

PICKING UP THE (FINANCIAL) PIECES

Douglas M. Lynch, CPA, CFA, CFP®

Doug is the president and chief compliance officer of Lynch Financial Group LLC. Lynch Financial Group is a fee-only registered investment advisor located in Dublin, OH that specializes in providing wealth management services to retirees and surviving spouses. A graduate of The Ohio State University, with a double major in accounting and finance, Doug became a certified public accountant (CPA) in 1992, a Chartered Financial Analyst® (CFA) in 1995, and a CERTIFIED FINANCIAL PLANNER™ professional (CFP®) in 2014. He is a member of The National Association of Personal Financial Advisors (NAPFA), Financial Planning Association, CFA Institute, and CFA Society of Columbus.

LIFE SOMETIMES THROWS us curve balls we could never see coming. Molly was a 43-year-old stay-at-home mom when her husband John was diagnosed with cancer that progressed very rapidly. He passed away within months of his diagnosis. Molly's immediate concerns were her two young children and dealing with her grief—during a global pandemic. But there were a multitude of other looming issues:

investing life insurance proceeds, Social Security, medical insurance, taxes, making sure her estate planning documents were updated, whether to go back to work, etc. She contacted us to help her deal with those issues so she could focus on her family.

GETTING STARTED

Things had been fairly comfortable financially while John was alive and Molly wasn't particularly involved in the family's finances beyond the checking account. Now, "Will we be okay?" was the big question facing her. Fortunately, the answer appeared to be "yes." John had taken out two life insurance policies (although one was being questioned, as he had switched from one type of policy to another shortly before his illness) and they also had some retirement account savings.

Molly had plenty on her plate with home schooling of her children (partly due to the Covid-19 pandemic) and everything else that follows the death of a spouse. She didn't have the time, interest, or expertise in tackling all the financial matters that needed to be addressed on her own. However, there were some immediate steps that did need to be tackled:

- Applying for Social Security benefits. (The benefits for her two young children and her own survivor benefits would provide a decent base to cover part of their living expenses until the children were 18.)
- File claims for the two life insurance policies.
- Come up with a game plan for medical insurance for her family.

As a financial advisor, we often sit down with new clients to develop a detailed long-term financial plan. In Molly's case, however, it made more sense to tackle things in several stages over the coming years— taking care of the immediate needs and then focusing on other areas depending on their importance. This was because of the significant time involved in the near-term issues as well as the fact that some of the longer-term considerations were still unknowns (what their "new normal" living expenses would be, would Molly go back to work, where would they live, etc.) Also, only a month after the death of her husband, she had more important things to address than consulting with her insurance professionals to see if she had the right level of home and auto coverage.

INITIAL DECISIONS

An often-stated rule of thumb is for a widow not to make any large or significant decisions soon after the death of a spouse. This is good advice to a certain extent, since it takes time to get to the point of being able to tackle something other than just getting through the day emotionally. However, it also ignores some realities of life.

Life insurance claims should be made as soon as possible. Molly stated that she knew little about investments, but we agreed that she should be actively involved in decisions in this area. After she felt comfortable, we reviewed the historical risks and returns of different asset classes and came up with an initial game plan on investing her life insurance and retirement accounts. Molly told us that she wanted to invest wisely but did not want to take undue risk. Because the life insurance proceeds had not been previously invested, it was decided those amounts would be gradually phased in. Historically, on average, it is better to invest a lump sum all at once, as markets go up more often than they go down. Molly, however, isn't an average; she is a single dot on the graph of historical returns and is at a time in her life when erring on the side of safety makes more sense than trying to maximize returns. We agreed that once Molly became more comfortable with investments, we would revisit the initial decisions (level of risk, etc.) to see if they continue to make sense.

Medical insurance was another significant issue that needed to be addressed sooner rather than later. The coverage provided from her husband's employer would be ending and the family needed medical insurance going forward. COBRA coverage was available for a relatively short period of time through her husband's employer, but it was expensive. An alternative was to get a policy through the Affordable Care Act (ACA) exchange. Since Molly's income would be low while she wasn't working (her children's Social Security benefits are not included in the income calculation), tax credits would cover a large part of the cost of a policy through the exchange, so that was a better alternative. It was recommended that Molly find a good local professional who deals with these policies to help her through that process. With much more pressing things to deal with, Molly had to battle the federal bureaucracy's constant requests for information (some of which could not be known with any degree of precision, such as expected income, etc.)

NEXT STEPS

Housing is an area often cited in that rule of thumb advising against making big decisions for a while after the death of a spouse. However, in Molly's case, her family had moved to an apartment primarily because it was close to where John was treated. After John passed, Molly did not want to stay in the apartment, as it only held memories of John's illness and they had no other ties to it. Molly wanted to purchase a house. After we reviewed her financial situation, Molly decided to purchase a house that fit her family's needs, was in a school district she liked, and worked for her financially. After moving in, Molly said that she felt like they were making progress in the family's new stage of life.

Molly was unsure of whether she wanted or needed to go back to work. An intelligent young lady with a college degree in the medical profession, she had not worked for a number of years. While her children were younger, Molly expressed that she wanted to be there for them more than she wanted to go back to work. We discussed this and decided no big decision should be made immediately. Working didn't fit with her current desire to be home with her children and it potentially would decrease both her Social Security benefits and the tax credits on their medical insurance, which acted like a significant additional tax on any earnings from employment. This was an area to revisit in the future.

Taxes are not a subject a typical person finds interesting. Taxes, however, are one of the largest expenses in many households. It was important to minimize taxes where possible (ACA tax credits, IRA distribution planning, etc.) This was an area for which Molly was all too happy to outsource the planning to someone else.

As we talked about her expenses and goals, it became clear that Molly had a desire to make charitable donations. Her church was very important to the family, and she wanted to continue to support it. We talked about a way to fulfill that desire as well as honor her late husband. It was recommended she contribute shares of a stock that had performed very well recently to a charitable fund (a donor advised fund). This avoided recognizing a taxable gain (she did not want to keep the stock) and provided a tax deduction. The fund was named in her husband's memory. Molly was very happy with fulfilling both her charitable desires and being able to honor her husband at the same time.

Molly had a general idea of the different financial accounts she and John had. John had moved around to several jobs in several states during his life and had retirement accounts remaining at his current and previous employers. Unfortunately, Molly did not have login information for these and other accounts. This is a good reminder that in addition to "normal" estate documents, it's important to consider a "digital" estate plan to make sure both spouses have access to what accounts are established as well as login info. Molly had to do a fair amount of detective work to track down the various accounts. Many phone calls were made to companies, accompanied by plenty of requests for account paperwork, death certificates, etc.

Estate planning is not a favorite topic for most individuals—

perhaps even less so for someone who just went through the loss of a spouse. That said, we discussed that this is an area that should be addressed right away. A simple will for a young couple should take into account a worst-case scenario, but typically assumes one spouse will be around to take care of things if the other passes away. Molly's priority was to make sure she had a good plan in place for who would take care of her children and that they would be taken care of financially in the event of her own (hopefully very unlikely) death. We recommended Molly consult with family and friends and find a good local attorney who focuses on estate planning.

TO BE CONTINUED

As previously mentioned, we left some areas of her financial life to discuss in the coming years. We did a rough projection of her financial future to make some immediate decisions (can I afford to buy this house, etc.), but we understood that detailed projections couldn't really be made until her family had some time to see what their new life was like. With someone as young as Molly, the only certainty after developing a financial plan is that it will change over time but setting a baseline plan is extremely important. Reviewing areas like insurance and college education funding and having general discussions about how her investments are doing will become a part of more normal future meetings.

Financial advisors can get a bad rap (often well deserved), but Molly's story encapsulates well the value an advisor can provide to someone who really needs quality financial assistance at an important time in their life. Molly had more than enough on her plate dealing with the aftermath of John's death as well as the needs of her two children as a now-single parent. Trying to navigate the complexities of the items mentioned above on her own would be a huge burden outside her area of expertise (just as it would be for me to try to evaluate a medical issue Molly would be able to handle given her training).

Molly thanked us on numerous occasions for taking much of the financial stress off her plate and said that it "was so nice to be able to focus on what matters" (her children, dealing with her grief, etc.) The pandemic years 2020–2021 were difficult and stressful years for so many people due to health, employment, and general uncertainty reasons. For Molly to make it through that, while also overcoming the loss of a spouse and come out having done a phenomenal job of being a mom, was a blessing to be involved with.

IN SUMMARY

- An often-stated rule of thumb is for a widow not to make any large or significant decisions soon after the death of a spouse, but sometimes the realities of life don't allow for that.
- Consider a digital estate plan, to make sure both spouses have access to what accounts are established as well as login info.

THE POWER
TO PRESERVE

OPTIMIZING YOUR ASSETS TO FIND FINANCIAL PEACE

Simon A. Tryzna, CFA

Simon A. Tryzna, CFA, is a portfolio manager and financial advisor at Palo Alto Wealth Advisors. He is an expert in financial planning around concentrated equity positions and primarily works with clients with stock option equity compensation.

A proud graduate of Saint Mary's College, he enjoys mentoring students, especially those interested in pursuing a career in the finance industry. He has a passion for breaking down complicated financial planning and investment ideas into easy-to-digest language to help as many as possible.

Simon was formerly the chief investment officer at ClearPath Capital Partners, where he was featured in publications such as *The Wall Street Journal*, *Investment News*, and *Kiplinger's*. He enjoys collaborating with other advisors on educational pieces around investing and stock-option planning and writing about various financial planning and investment topics.

"I FEEL LIKE I'M living frugally, but every month I have to draw on my investments to make sure I have enough cash in my bank account for the next month."

One of the earliest lessons I learned about being a good financial advisor is the importance of actively listening to my clients. Rather than focusing on the words, it's crucial to focus on the delivery and contextualize it with everything we know about our clients.

I could feel the emotion in Ivan's voice through the phone.

In the years that I have known him, he has never been one to splurge on things. His one big purchase was a nice car, and he only did that with realized gains from his early investment in Bitcoin.

He estimated that he was spending roughly $100,000 more than he earned each year, and admitted that his monthly routine had begun to take a mental and emotional toll on him.

I was genuinely shocked to learn of his predicament.

THE BACKGROUND

Ivan was a computer engineer who played a crucial role in a couple of start-ups that had successful exits and was now a part of another up-and-coming business. He did consulting work on the side and was always on top of his finances. We managed his liquid assets, provided guidance, and helped coordinate things with his accountant wherever necessary. We never did any formal financial planning work for him.

This dynamic remained true after his divorce a few years ago. There were a lot of changes in his life around that time, and aside from providing counseling whenever requested, I tended to let Ivan be. He knew what he was doing when it came to balancing his income and expenses. Despite multiple offerings to do active financial planning for him, I never had the opportunity to help him in more detail. Now here he was taking me up on my offer.

Here was my chance to help him.

IDENTIFYING THE PROBLEM

Ivan and I agreed that the first step in becoming cash-flow positive was to do a deep dive into understanding his income and expenses. While this could be a daunting task, he already had a solid understanding of both of those. Following our call, he entered all of his information into our financial planning software, where I could look at the data alongside him.

The numbers jumped out at both of us. The majority of his expenses were in three categories: alimony, child support, and mortgage payments. His remaining spending was in line with what I knew about him—the hallmark of someone who was frugal and didn't live an expensive lifestyle.

As we talked through his cash flows, he told me about the sadness he had going into his bank account every month to send his ex-wife the payments and the emotional toll it took on him.

The challenge was now twofold—what if we could alleviate the cash-flow problem but do it in such a way that relieved Ivan of the monthly stress?

PAINTING THE PICTURE

Now that Ivan and I had a good grasp of his cash-flow situation, the next step was to understand his balance sheet fully. While Ivan was a diligent saver, I was afraid that he might have been underutilizing his assets, and I wanted to see if there was something that we could do to help him with his cash-flow problem.

To get an idea of his whole financial picture, Ivan and I put together a brand-new balance sheet to get an up-to-date snapshot of his finances.

It looked straightforward. Ivan had an approximately $2.2m portfolio (comprising taxable and retirement assets), as well as a $1.8m house. His house had a pretty high mortgage balance ($1.5m) and a

4.125% interest rate, which equated to Ivan's high monthly mortgage payments and contributed to his cash-flow problems.

While he did have a solid equity compensation package at his latest start-up, there was no pathway for an income raise in the near future. However, what Ivan did have, which surprised me, was a highly appreciated crypto-asset position that had ballooned to $3.5 million, despite his monthly sales.

I knew he was interested in crypto and had been allocating some of his savings into it, but I never imagined it being the size that it was. With the massive appreciation of Ivan's position over the previous few years, combined with the divorce cutting his assets in half, the position in crypto had suddenly become the most significant asset on his balance sheet.

WHY WE INVEST

One of the most important things I tell my clients is that we need to have a purpose behind our investments. We invest the excess cash—the cash left over from our income after paying off our expenses. Excess cash is the by-product of being cash-flow positive and being cash-flow positive is something that Ivan excelled in before his divorce.

We invest to grow our excess cash to use it at a later point in time, and we invest so we have more money to spend on vacations, retirement, college, home purchase, and emergencies. And while Ivan was no longer saving, he did have assets built up from diligent saving throughout his life.

So, when he needed to supplement his income with cash, he did the right thing by tapping into his crypto position, which was a by-product of diligent saving (and smart investing) over the previous few years.

As we looked at his balance sheet holistically, I realized that we could make his large crypto position work in his favor more efficiently than he was currently utilizing it. Ivan did a phenomenal job of building that up, and it was my job to guide him in using that position to help him meet his latest goals.

His trimming his crypto position slowly, on a month-by-month basis, was not the most efficient use of it. He was undertaking a lot of risk by having the bulk of his balance sheet in crypto—a risky asset. Even though both Ivan and I felt that it was an excellent investment, we both realized just how much risk he had.

FIGURING OUT THE SOLUTION

In looking at the situation at hand, the best thing I could do to help Ivan was to ensure that he felt he had an ample amount in the bank and didn't feel forced into selling his crypto to help make ends meet. My challenge was working with him to optimize his hard-earned assets and make sure they worked as efficiently as possible to help him live his desired life.

Ivan's crypto position as a percentage of his net worth was a lot higher than he had ever anticipated it being. His $3.5m position far outweighed the $300,000 in equity he had in his home. After a conversation with my mortgage broker, Ivan and I realized that he could cut his monthly mortgage payment from $7,500 to $3,675. That's an annualized saving of almost $46,000.

To cut down the mortgage payment, we would need to increase equity in his home. For Ivan, the easiest way to do that would be to trim his crypto holdings and use the proceeds to pay down the mortgage principal. Over a few weeks, Ivan sold $750,000 of his position and used it to pay down his existing mortgage. We then worked with our broker to refinance it and get his rate down to 3.5%.

One of his larger monthly expenditures was slashed by a little more than half, and his balance sheet looked a lot better with decreased crypto exposure and higher equity in his home.

A NEGATIVE EXTERNALITY

A significant drawback in selling a highly appreciated asset is the capital gains tax liability that's now due. Even though it would be taxed at long-term capital gains rates (which are less than ordinary income rates), Ivan was now facing a hefty tax bill.

In solving one of the pain points, we created a new one. While there is no getting around paying Uncle Sam, different solutions are available to potentially help offset taxes. When it comes to realized capital gains, the most common way to offset them is by having realized capital losses. This is commonly done by "harvesting losses," a method popular with investors, who sell their investments at a loss and use those losses to negate the gains.

A solution that looks to continually harvest losses is a customized direct indexing program that has a restriction of zero capital gains.

I explained to Ivan that the breadth of returns of individual stocks in the S&P 500 makes a customized direct indexing strategy appealing as a tax optimization solution. The program can mimic the returns and risk profile of the S&P 500 by investing in 130–150 stocks. Given that not all stocks appreciate simultaneously, the program can harvest losses on an ongoing basis, whether it is daily, monthly, or quarterly. The benefit to the investor is that they could have exposure to the S&P 500 while actively harvesting losses to offset the realized capital gain of their stock or, in Ivan's case, his crypto position.

Operationally, a customized direct indexing strategy requires the funding of an account co-managed by the index provider. Such an account could also have a recurring monthly Automated Clearing House (ACH) payment out of it, where each month, a set amount of cash would be sent out without the account holder needing to do anything.

THE GAME PLAN

Combining the benefit of having a tax-optimized account that continually harvests losses with the fact that we could set up automated payments to his ex-wife, I came to Ivan with the following proposal:

Fund a separate account that would be in a direct indexing strategy.

1. Sell an additional $500,000 of crypto to fund the account and set it up to harvest losses whenever possible.
2. Set up the program within the account so that there is enough cash available to be automatically sent out to his ex-wife for alimony and child support each month. He wouldn't need to do anything or think about it—I'd work with the appropriate parties to ensure this got done the way I designed it.
3. Doing this would help him further divest out of his crypto. Even with the monthly cash outlay, it was still possible for the account to appreciate. Should the equity market continue to appreciate at a high enough rate, there would be the possibility of the account having funds remaining once his alimony and child support payments concluded.

He loved this idea and was all-in.

EXECUTION

Over the course of about three months, Ivan and I were able to work with our mortgage broker, custodian, and index provider, to get all of this set up. Once the plan was put in place, the execution was relatively straightforward.

But the end product of this was huge.

Ivan accomplished his primary goal of improving his cash flows. Not only that, he did so in a way that de-risked his overall financial portfolio (by divesting his crypto position and re-investing it in his house and the U.S. equity market). And, more importantly, it allowed him the peace of mind to not think about his divorce on a monthly basis.

A few months after our plan was executed, I had lunch with Ivan. It was my first time seeing him in person in a little over a year due to the Covid-19 pandemic. Immediately I could tell that he was in a much better headspace. He was excited to tell me about all the positive things going on in his life: his new relationship, how things were progressing with his company, and the planned trips he had on the horizon. With his cash-flow situation fixed, he was back to saving and investing and was educating me on all of the latest happenings in the crypto universe.

After we finished our lunch, I was ecstatic to hear how things were going for Ivan. I was amazed at how impactful a well-executed financial plan can be on someone's life. It was really good to have the old Ivan back.

IN SUMMARY

- We need to have a purpose behind our investments.

HIGH EARNERS, NOT WEALTHY...YET

Jordan Benold

Jordan Benold is co-owner of Benold Financial Planning with his father. He is a fee-only financial planner in Frisco, TX serving clients in Texas. He specializes in helping physicians with financial planning. His father, uncle and both grandfathers were physicians.

"**W**HAT IS GOING on?" Amber exclaimed, looking at her bank statement from last month. It was lower than the previous month. Next, she opened her statement from two months prior.

"I give up. Why do our accounts keep going down instead of up?"

Amber, 46, decided to start auditing the family's finances to see why they were not saving money. Her husband Shane, 48, has a great job as a family physician, and she works as the chief of staff for a local politician. Her income did not compare to his, as Shane was making a significant salary. But they were in this as a team. With her hands in her hair, she decided to call her husband at work.

TROUBLE IN PARADISE?

"Hello, Amber, is something wrong?" Shane asked.

"Yes, do you know what would be causing our bank accounts to decrease over the last few months? It sure looks to me like we are overspending and not saving enough."

"Amber, I make plenty of money. You make decent money. How could our bank accounts be decreasing? That does not make sense."

"Ugh, I don't know, but I think we should hire someone to help us sort this out. Lauren's been raving about her financial planner for years. Why don't we give him a call?"

Shane replied, "We don't need a financial planner. Most of them are just cheats, liars, and salesmen pretending to be your best friend. Look, we both contribute to our 401(k)s, we put money in our investment accounts, and we still have plenty of money to go on vacations. We live a great life."

"Well, yeah, but I'd still like to get a second opinion."

Shane didn't agree with Amber, but he knew that she was coming from a place of caring and safety.

"Okay," he said, "But you run with it. I'm super busy."

A few days later, I received a phone call from Amber.

LIVING LIFE LARGE

How is it that a 40-something couple with ample income were falling behind? As Amber correctly guessed, the problem wasn't complicated. At any income level, if you routinely spend more than you earn, it's unlikely you'll end up wealthy. It's just that simple.

Some people, like Amber, will quickly become unhappy about being behind the proverbial eight ball. Others, like Shane, may not mind at first. But "out of sight, out of mind" has a way of catching up with you eventually. Either way, overspending rarely leads to happy endings.

So, what did Amber and Shane really want out of life? As we dived into that conversation, lightbulbs started blinking on for both of them. Both hoped to retire on the young side. But they also had two kids to put through college. In the meantime, they were living life large—working hard, for sure, but playing hard too. They were "foodies," who enjoyed dining out, gourmet groceries, and their pricey daily coffee and tea drinks. They took lavish vacations—four trips annually in the U.S. and abroad. Theatre, more dining, Caribbean beaches and European adventures.

On top of all that, they were carrying heavy consumer debt: student loans, a home equity loan, an automobile loan, and some high-interest credit card debt. Oh, and then there was that Disney timeshare they were still paying off.

BRINGING UP THE "B" WORD (BUDGET)

After we tallied it all up, it seemed clear. Amber and Shane had some challenging choices ahead of them. For that, they would need a monthly budget to guide the way.

By then, I'd learned some of Amber's body language as well. I could almost feel her relaxing into the idea with a small smile and a nearly inaudible sigh of relief.

Shane, on the other hand, fell silent, arms crossed, eyes cast downward. Shane was not smiling.

He didn't say it out loud, but I knew what he was thinking: "Budgets are for cash-strapped people with money problems, not for me."

That said, one of Shane's finer qualities was that he was always willing to listen, even when he didn't necessarily agree.

"When do you want to stop working?" I asked them.

They agreed their late 50s or early 60s would be ideal. They'd both seen their parents work much longer at labor-intensive jobs, and they didn't want that to happen to them.

I asked if they wanted to maintain their current lifestyle in retirement. Of course, they said yes.

Then, we ran the actual numbers. Comparing their spending goals to their assets, income, investments, retirement plan savings, etc. Those numbers didn't lie. They would have to work into their 70s.

Talk about a wake-up call. With that, they were both all-in. Amber and Shane both exclaimed that they wanted to change their current lifestyle and reduce expenses, so they could enjoy retirement worry-free. After detailed guidance on how to get going, they went home, opened a bottle of wine, and created their first family budget.

INFORMED DECISIONS, CHALLENGING CHOICES

While budgeting and planning aren't necessarily easy tasks, they are made easier by realizing how essential they are to enjoying what wealth you have across the spectrum of your life. Without planning, it's easy to get caught up in the daily fray, spending on every little thing, instead of on what truly adds value to your life.

In that context, Shane and Amber started sorting through their spending.

To get a grip on the spending, we identified three main "suspects" to cross-examine: their debt load, their fondness for fine foods, and their lavish vacations.

The food plans were perhaps the easiest. They both agreed to buy more groceries at lower-cost grocery stores and have more meals at home instead of eating out. They each agreed to make their coffees and teas at home.

Next, the vacations. By cutting their adventures to one family trip and one splashier "just the two of us" trip each year, they could really take a bite out of their outgoing cash flow. This would free up money to save and invest toward future adventures.

Eliminating their consumer debt load was a bigger, but important nut to crack. We put our collective heads together and worked through a plan for doing just that by using their belt-tightening cash flow to get the job done. The painfully high-interest credit card debt had to come first, as it was the biggest drag on their wealth. Then came the Disney timeshare, the lower-interest student loans, the car loan, and finally, the home equity loan. With a timetable in place and a sweet cash-flow light at the end of the tunnel, Shane and Amber were able to pay off all their consumer debt in under two years, leaving them with only their home mortgage.

With their debt paid off, they could then focus that same cash flow on their future goals. Again, the specific numbers don't matter as much as their strategy to kick their own retirement savings and their children's college savings into much higher gear. They also started building up an emergency fund to ward off life's unexpected curve balls.

A CHORE BECOMES AN ADVENTURE

Shane and Amber soon found themselves surprisingly enthusiastic about their new financial planning protocols. At first, especially for Shane, all that budgeting, saving, and planning had felt foreign, formidable, and forbidding. But there's something liberating about knowing what the future has in store for your money. After paying down their debt, ramping up their savings and investing, and still having monthly positive cash flow to enjoy, they decided they'd like to pay off that home mortgage as well. After additional planning, they resolved to knock out their 30-year loan over the next 12 years. This would save them substantial interest, which, to their delight, would provide them even more cash flow for future expenditures such as a new car, extra vacations, and, with any luck, glorious weddings for their children.

Recently, I asked Shane and Amber if they had any advice to share with other hard-working high-earners who might think they're too busy, or don't need to budget, save, or invest. They both quickly replied, "If we can do it, anyone else can too!"

I'm pleased to report that Shane and Amber are now not just high earners, but are also well on their way to being wealthy.

IN SUMMARY

- Budgets aren't just for cash-strapped people with money problems. They are for everyone!
- Budgets do not constrain you; they liberate you.

WHAT MATTERS MOST

Steven Fox, CFP®, EA

Steven Fox is the founder of Next Gen Financial Planning in San Diego, a fee-only firm helping young professionals with investing, tax planning, student loans, and other areas of financial planning.

He is an active member of the Financial Planning Association (and has served as president of the San Diego chapter) and the National Association of Personal Financial Advisors. Steven was also the treasurer and volunteer coordinator for Financial Independence Training, a volunteer organization that provided financial planning to active duty Marines and sailors.

"WE MAKE GREAT income now, why is all this money stuff still so hard?"

My exasperated new clients, Nadira and her husband Carlos, sat across my conference table, frustrated that no matter how hard they worked there never seemed to be enough money available.

They had indeed come quite a long way already, though still early in their careers at the ages of 32 and 34. Both had overcome immense challenges to get to where they were in life. Between the two of them they had endured crushing poverty, years of domestic abuse, physical illnesses, the loss of close family members, multiple miscarriages, and entanglement within a violent gang. They had not merely survived these trials but sculpted themselves into resilient and well-accomplished professionals who were now excelling at all of the things they were told to do in order to be "successful." They were determined to end the negative cycles that they had been born into.

Nadira had willed her way into a highly competitive business program at a leading university and graduated near the top of her class, despite being the first in her family to go to college. She was now a thriving junior executive at a widely admired national marketing firm, crafting compelling stories for major brands. Nadira was well on her way into what she considered to be the career of her dreams, allowing her to exercise both the creative and technical sides of her brain while making her family proud.

Carlos had immigrated to the United States as a teenager and did not go to college, but worked his way through self-directed online training programs to learn how to become a software developer. He was now leading a team of developers at a prominent start-up working to create software to help hospitals integrate diagnostic equipment. This career felt worlds away from the wide-ranging jobs of his past that included stints as a drug dealer, tattoo artist, and grocery store clerk.

Both were clearly driven and brilliant people, and as often occurs in my line of work, I was tremendously impressed with my new clients. But despite all the progress that they had made in life and financially, they were still every bit as stressed about money as they had ever been. They had fallen into the common trap of believing that working hard and increasing their incomes would magically make all of their problems go away and were now realizing that it was going to take something more.

NEW COMPLEXITIES

As we started digging into the details of their financial situation and organizing everything, it quickly became clear that we had some important questions to answer together. Some examples of the challenges that they were facing included:

- How much should they be saving for the future, and in which types of accounts?
- How should they decide what to invest in?
- How did Carlos' employer stock options work?
- What was their best way to save for college for their one-year-old son, Nico?
- What kind of life insurance should they get?
- Should they prioritize paying off Nadira's large student loan balance of $290,000?
- Would they be able to buy a house, and how much should they spend on it?

These are all common questions that people (rightfully) expect a qualified financial planner to help them answer. But beyond these surface-level quantitative and analytical issues, I got the sense that both Nadira and Carlos were becoming deeply unhappy with their lives and that their most important questions weren't solvable with spreadsheets and charts. After all that they had overcome and earning around $300,000 per year doing work that they found challenging and rewarding, they still felt unsettled and overwhelmed by everything financial. They also had a negative net worth that was trending even worse, argued frequently about spending, and tended to ignore financial topics until circumstances forced a change.

One particular point of conflict between them was Nadira's student loans. They had been paying the minimum required amount under an income-driven repayment plan for several years, which meant that her balance had actually grown since graduation because of the accrued interest. Their recent marriage meant that Carlos' income would now also be included in the calculation of the required monthly payment amount, which they only recently realized would soon be more than doubling. Carlos wanted to pay back the loans aggressively, but Nadira felt guilty about using their joint money to pay them off when Carlos didn't even go to college, and she resented creating even just the appearance of her being "rescued" by a man.

Another area in which they struggled to align was how to manage their spending. Both of them recognized that even though their income had risen dramatically over the past few years, their spending had gone right up alongside the raises and they were still somehow anxiously awaiting every paycheck to pay off the credit card bills. They had fallen prey to lifestyle inflation, emulating the luxury purchases of their coworkers and friends while justifying it to themselves as having been earned by their hard work and assuming that they could make up for it by saving more later in life. Both tended to just make purchases on the fly without any pre-planning or consulting each other, which created frequent conflict. They had tried various types of budgeting systems and apps, but none lasted for more than a couple of weeks before they gave up.

Most of all, Nadira was beginning to resent her time spent at work because it took away from being with their son. She had taken two months of maternity leave when he was born but returned to work as soon as she could because she was worried about the financial impact of an extended loss of income. As time went on, she grew more concerned with losing the fleeting opportunity to spend time with Nico while he was so young and felt guilty about dropping him off at daycare for somebody else to watch him each workday. Her previous miscarriages weighed heavily, and she thought she'd never forgive herself for that missed time if the worst were to happen.

A CLARITY BREAKTHROUGH

It's a tricky thing, trying to ask a client what their goals are for their financial plan and their life. It's a necessary step of course, to know what targets we're aiming for, but to ask the question outright often leads to the same shallow answers. Few individuals, and even fewer couples, proactively take the time to try to clearly define what they want life to look like in the future and to then tie that specific vision to the financial decisions they make in the present. Sitting down with a financial planner to discuss the future can sometimes be the spark that lights up the opportunity to make that connection.

I've heard from several other financial planners, and have often felt myself, that we are really just unqualified therapists or marriage counselors who happen to be additionally armed with spreadsheets. Tears are fairly common in my office, as are fierce sideways glances between couples expecting me to mediate a point of dispute. I knew that with Nadira and Carlos, no amount of investment analysis or student loan strategy discussions or tax return reviews would ever truly make an impact on their lives unless connected to something more.

During one of our first few meetings while onboarding them as clients and creating the initial version of their financial plan, I cautiously but confidently recommended that they also seek out a therapist. No professional therapist would ever share with me the private discussions they'd had with our mutual client, but I was hopeful that counseling would help this couple gain clarity about what they really wanted in life and what was holding them back from accomplishing it. They acknowledged that they'd already been considering a therapist, and seemed nearly ready to get started.

As our work together progressed, it became clear that Nadira really did want to go on an extended sabbatical for a few years to spend more time with Nico, but her and Carlos both immediately dismissed the idea as infeasible because she was earning nearly half of their income. With the combined pressures of other financial priorities like paying off student loans, saving for retirement, supporting their parents when needed, and buying a home for their growing family (with San Diego housing prices during a pandemic, no less!), she felt completely trapped.

A GLIMPSE OF LIGHT

If you ask a financial planner a question about money, their answer is likely to begin with "it depends." This can of course be tremendously frustrating to the one asking, but it really is true. And that's because personal finance is just that: personal. There are some financial decisions that could be universally regarded as bad, but probably none that can be universally agreed upon as good. So when Nadira asked me if it were in fact possible for her to take a sabbatical from work for a few years, my response was simply to give her a challenge: "If I say yes, will you do it?"

With a first glance at the numbers, it seemed obvious that losing Nadira's income of $130,000 for a few years until Nico began kindergarten would be a big setback. Her income was more than high enough to cover the cost of daycare, and they were already stretched tight on cash flow each month. But a closer look at the details helped us to uncover that the long-term financial impact of taking that time off was much smaller than it initially seemed.

By switching to a different type of student loan repayment plan that omitted Carlos' income and filing taxes separately, they could keep Nadira's student loan payments down to zero and aim for maximizing a loan forgiveness program over time rather than aggressively paying it off as fast as possible. Consolidating a few other debts into one with a lower rate could lower the total interest cost and put them on a clearly defined timeline to payoff.

Carlos was able to sell his accumulated shares from the employee stock purchase plan that he'd been automatically enrolled in and continue regularly doing so from that point on to help improve cash flow. He could also reduce exercises of his employee stock options, many of which weren't set to expire until as much as ten years out and were illiquid and risky in the meantime.

Aimlessly bouncing around to different budgeting apps in the midst of never-ending lifestyle inflation had led only to more stress, so they committed to a clear spending plan together and created a system of separate accounts with designated purposes and automated transfers. This required some tough and direct conversations with each other to gain clarity around what it was they were really saving for.

There were also a few less obvious opportunities to lower costs, such as replacing their expensive and unnecessary whole life insurance policies with much simpler term policies. They also reduced some expenses that they didn't even realize they were paying on the investments that they'd built up so far, and were able to keep more of what their accounts earned.

Through a series of small and achievable actions like these, it was becoming clear that this seemingly impossible goal might indeed be within their grasp. Quick wins taken one step at a time helped Carlos and Nadira develop confidence that they would be able to find their way through.

BEYOND NUMBERS

Some might argue that being a stay-at-home parent is a poor financial decision. If financial success is measured by net worth, then there's a reasonable case to be made there (though it's not always true). But if money is instead viewed as a tool for accomplishing the things that are most important in life rather than a scorecard or a proxy for ego, and if we make decisions to optimize for living in accord with our deepest values rather than optimizing for spreadsheets, we can find much deeper fulfillment and have greater confidence in our financial decisions.

A balance sheet doesn't have to be limited to what we traditionally think of as assets and liabilities. Why not include values for time with the kids and the opportunity to do emotionally fulfilling work on the asset side, or include the mental burdens of high debt and time spent in a frustrating daily commute on the liabilities side? A "good" or "bad" financial decision might quickly swing in the other direction once the real costs and benefits are all accounted for.

Nadira and Carlos had the vision, courage, and clarity to transform their lives through acting on the plan we created together. The magic was not in my set of recommendations or technical expertise around any financial planning areas, it was in Nadira's and Carlos' willingness to come together and move decisively in the direction that they knew to be right for their family. A written financial plan accompanied by charts and graphs outlining expectations for the coming years do have some small value by themselves, but going through a thoughtful financial planning process that puts people first can be absolutely transformative. I simply gave them the tools to make more informed decisions, and let them do the rest.

"All this money stuff" that has the potential to bring Nadira and Carlos (or nearly any of us mere humans) almost to their breaking points can also serve us in our efforts to build more meaningful lives. If there is any single universal truth I've learned in my career as a financial planner, it's that the best financial decisions are the ones aligned with a clear vision about what we're truly working towards in life. We are not automatically doomed or blessed into the cycles that we were born into, and the power to change the future is ours if we dare to use it.

IN SUMMARY

- Being a financial planner can feel like being an unqualified therapist or marriage counselor who happens to be additionally armed with spreadsheets.
- A balance sheet doesn't have to be limited to what we traditionally think of as assets and liabilities. It can include the practical and emotional results of financial decisions.

THE
POWER TO
CELEBRATE

WHAT THE HAT LADY OF HOLLYWOOD TAUGHT US

Andrew Martz, CFP®, MBA

Andrew Martz is a husband, father, and financial planner. He is the Founder & President of WIS Advisors, a comprehensive planning firm serving the sports and entertainment industries with offices in Los Angeles, Dallas, and Denver. He is also the co-host of Dollars & Sensibilities, a weekly podcast that discusses the numbers, concepts, and behaviors that shape financial decision-making. Andrew is a member of the DFW chapter of the Financial Planning Association. He is a CERTIFIED FINANCIAL PLANNER™ professional and holds an MBA in Financial Planning. WIS Advisors Inc. is not affiliated with Western International Securities. Securities and advisory services are offered through Western International Securities Inc., Member FINRA/SIPC.

I'LL NEVER FORGET when I first met Ms Charlotte Bauer of Hollywood, California. She was a widow in her 80s, and had been referred to our office for financial and banking services. From the instant she breezed in, it was as if all of Tinseltown had swept through our office door.

"Feel my arm!" she offered, as she introduced herself, and flexed her strong right bicep for us to examine. "Not bad for an old lady, eh?"

As I learned over time, Charlotte was always mid-story like that. With every visit, she would state her business, and then quickly launch in: "Oh, Andrew, you'll never believe what Henry just said," or, "Guess what? 409 is late with their rent again…"

Never mind that we had no idea who Henry was, or which apartment 409 she was referring to.

Of course, that was part of her charm, and why everyone in the office would stop by to say hello whenever Charlotte was around. You never wanted to miss a thing about her.

THEN THERE WERE THE HATS

An Austrian who'd escaped the Nazi regime by immigrating to the U.S. as a young woman, Charlotte Bauer was the quintessential Grande Dame of Hollywood—hard knocks and big dreams combined. Even in busy, bustling Hollywood, Charlotte Bauer was someone you'd soon notice, and long remember.

"Casual day" didn't exist in her world. It was as if she'd read Queen Elizabeth II's playbook, and then improved on it. She would visit with us nearly weekly (often before or after her daily swims), and she always arrived in a different smartly tailored dress, skirt and blouse, or pantsuit. Each ensemble would be a single solid—from bright yellow, to dark green, to pastel pink—complemented by an immaculate piece of matching jewelry. No garish prints or clashing patterns for Charlotte.

Then there were the hats. Charlotte always wore a hat and it always perfected the rest of her outfit.

"Hat Lady is here!" we would beam, as Ms Bauer came to call.

But make no mistake, while those hats were a big part of her persona, heaven help you if you failed to realize they were protecting one of the sharpest minds you'd ever meet.

Despite her soft voice and motherly demeanor, she was a businesswoman through and through. She could rival any Fortune 500 CEO with her swift decisions, fair but firm.

In short, Ms Bauer was as savvy as she was sophisticated, perhaps in part because she adored being in the thick of every story.

LARGER THAN LIFE

Charlotte rarely spoke about her own past. She didn't want to "be a bother." She preferred to spin out marvelous tales about the people around her. You could divide the cast of characters in her life into roughly three groups (and then try to keep up as she narrated their many adventures).

First, there were her property people. Ms Bauer owned buildings throughout Hollywood and elsewhere in California. She and her late husband had acquired many of them not long after he had retired from his medical practice. After her husband passed, Charlotte carried on, spending her days managing property managers, and collecting and depositing rent checks. As you might imagine, there were countless tales to be told, with one intrigue melding into the next. She would also describe the endless escapades in the high-rise condo where she lived and socialized with fellow residents of all ages and stripes.

The next group was her business associates and advisors. At least in Charlotte's eyes, every one of us was "the best." If she did business with an accountant, they weren't just bean-counters; they were miracle workers. Her real estate attorney was the most amazing lawyer ever. "You sure don't want to go up against him in court," she would exclaim.

She was never short on appreciation for our services. Of course, we aimed to offer excellent care to all our clients, but admittedly, you couldn't help but put an extra spring in your step when Charlotte was around.

The last, and by far the most important, person in Charlotte's life was her only son, Michael.

There was nothing in the world Ms Bauer was prouder of than her son. When he was a boy, she had taught him to speak English and German. She would remind us he had perfected the latter without a hint of an accent, but there was more to it than that. She and her husband had worked very hard, and hoped to instill the same ethic in their son. They never took for granted the labor, education, and life lessons that had contributed to their financial success.

WEALTH PRESERVATION FROM MOTHER TO CHILD

Charlotte Bauer was a first-generation wealth-builder. Experiencing poverty, hunger, and a life-altering journey at an early age, she had earned every bit of the grit and fortitude that would lead to her subsequent success.

That said, our country is populated by first generations with similar stories; less common is the ability to sustain that level of success. I've seen sources conservatively estimate that 70% of wealthy families will lose their wealth by the second generation and 90% will lose it by the third.

Fortunately for the second—and now third—generation of the Bauer family, there was nothing common about Charlotte. She had seen these same statistics, and wanted us to help her and her heirs beat the odds. This was among the driving forces that brought her through our door when she was already in her 80s.

Because Charlotte had mostly been a "do it yourself" money manager during her long life, there were several inheritance and tax-planning challenges already embedded into her legacy plans. Had she come to us sooner, we probably could have done more to manage the size of her estate and reduce some of its steep built-in gains. We were, however, able to talk at length about how we could best position Michael for future success.

BEATING THE GENERATIONAL ODDS

I met Michael Bauer and his wife Jacqueline a year or so after getting to know his mother. From our first conversation, we hit it off as well. Together, we spent a lot of time looking at their savings and spending patterns, independent of whether they inherited any family wealth. We agreed that this type of planning would allow them to consider best- and worst-case scenarios, giving them their best chance of beating those generational odds.

Early in his career, Michael had been an international banker, making good use of the language skills Charlotte had taught him when he was young. Then, in his early 50s, he had retired from banking, and he and his wife Jacqueline went into real estate for themselves.

When I spoke to Michael about his career path, he emphasized that he had charted his own way by watching his mother and father's example, rather than depending on their financial support. Michael and Jacqueline had made their first significant property acquisition from money they had diligently saved, along with a home equity loan on their personal residence. They proudly owned and operated an apartment complex they managed themselves—until a new challenge emerged.

Though the rental property created good income, it had taken away their freedom to fully enjoy their retirement, and do things they were passionate about, like travel. However, to get clean out of the daily property management grind, they were looking at a substantial, seven-figure capital gain bill. Neither could stomach paying that much in taxes.

Together, we were able to develop a passive business strategy that allowed them to sell the building to an active owner, while deferring taxes and continuing to receive an income stream. Freedom achieved. Wealth preserved.

INDEPENDENT THINKING

Speaking of family, Michael and Jacqueline had one child as well—their daughter, Emilia. Just as Charlotte's favorite subject had been her son, so too was Emilia the apple of her parents' eyes. Whenever we met, I would hear about her every move: her student achievements, her first job, her marriage to Richard, whom she'd met in high school and reconnected with later on.

When I eventually met with Emilia and Richard to discuss their financial plans, I once again saw that signature Bauer family grit shining through. By then, there was a fair amount of wealth to be bequeathed, and if Emilia and Richard received an inheritance, that would be great. But they weren't going to bank on it. Instead, since then we have been focusing on preserving their independent assets through strategies such as optimizing their tax-deferred and tax-free retirement income. We're also using Roth and backdoor Roth IRA contributions while we're able to offset the impact of any taxable inheritances they may receive.

In short, we are busy helping Charlotte's granddaughter make plans of her own. I never had the opportunity to meet Charlotte's late husband, but I'm sure he would have loved what he and his gutsy bride had inspired so many years ago.

HATS OFF TO A CELEBRATED LADY

One day I got the call none of us ever wants to receive. Charlotte Bauer had passed. Not surprisingly, her people gathered from near and far: her property people; her professional advisors; the residents in her tight-knit condo community; and, of course, her family. We all came together to celebrate the life of an incredible woman who had made such a positive impact on nearly everyone she encountered.

Perhaps the most important lesson a parent can pass to a child—or each of us can implement—is the attitude of gratitude. Success is not defined by the size of your bank account, but by the joy you give and take, as you make the most of what you've got. Ms Charlotte Bauer had embodied this life lesson, so it's no wonder anyone who had been privileged to know her wanted to bid her a bittersweet farewell. It's no wonder, as we gathered to honor her memory, we all wore our biggest, brightest hats, to celebrate what the Hat Lady of Hollywood had taught us all.

IN SUMMARY

- Even do-it-yourself money managers can benefit from expert advice, especially when transforming their wealth into their legacy.
- Success is not defined by the size of your bank account, but by the joy you give and take as you make the most of what you've got.

THE AMERICAN DREAM

Dana J. Menard, CFP®

Dana J. Menard, CFP®, RLP®, CEPA®, CDAA™ (he/him/his) is the founder and lead financial planner at Twin Cities Wealth Strategies, Inc., a fee-only, fiduciary financial planning firm located in the Minneapolis/St. Paul metro area. He helps guide career-focused professionals, entrepreneurs, and small business owners through a proven process to help them lead a life of purpose. He believes that everyone deserves *real* financial advice and not just to be sold financial products without first being thoroughly financially diagnosed. Dana is active in his local community and regularly volunteers his time in local schools educating students on financial literacy topics. He is frequently featured in both local and national financial news outlets.

LAURA AND DALE were frustrated. After being turned away by another large, well-known financial institution for not having enough "investable assets," they'd had just about enough. They grew increasingly disheartened during their months-long search for a financial advisor to help them put together a real financial plan. With each firm that pushed them aside, they became more and more discouraged. They worked hard and felt as if they were fairly successful as entrepreneurs and small business owners, causing their financial situation to become more complicated by the day.

Laura and Dale were a happily married couple in their early 50s. They were college sweethearts who now ran a successful digital marketing agency together, which allowed them to live a comfortable upper-middle-class life within the limits of the big city. They had three children: Ashley, Hannah, and Jacob. When we first spoke, Ashley was a freshman in college while Hannah and Jacob were still in high school.

For Laura and Dale, the autonomy of becoming their own bosses and owning their own business was how they defined achieving their "American Dream."

Dale mentioned that the standard notion of working for somebody else, earning a fixed salary with basic benefits, and having to set aside money regularly for retirement (hopefully) flew out the window once he and Laura established their own business. When they started their agency, it was founded with very little capital or funding. They were forced to bootstrap their business with their life savings and take on some debt, making it even more challenging to get ahead initially. But they had overcome the struggle and were just paying off the last of their debt. They had more discretionary income than ever before due to the agency's success.

Over the past 19 years, I've seen countless entrepreneurs in similar situations. They have started a business alone, and most focus on what they have been good at historically as technicians of their craft. While it usually works out in the short term, running the business *as a business* for the long term is much more difficult. It's no wonder that about 20% of new small businesses in the United States fail within the first year. Roughly 50% falter by the end of their fifth year, and after ten years, only about a third will have survived (see www.bls.gov/bdm/entrepreneurship/bdm_chart3.htm).

Aside from the early financial struggle, most business owners invest most, if not all, of their earnings back into their business, as reinvesting profits allows for business growth. They rarely conform to the savings philosophy that most salaried employees do. For most, their net worth is tied up in their business. For this reason, many financial advisors are quick to overlook entrepreneurs and small business owners because they don't have significant discretionary investable assets to manage. So, those who have more complicated situations and require more financial advice get overlooked.

Imagine, just for a moment, that you were ill and could not figure out what ailed you. Confused, you seek out a doctor to help diagnose the issue and prescribe a treatment plan to get you healthy. How would you feel if the doctor turned you away and told you to come back only once you were healthy? It seems counter-intuitive, doesn't it?

Sadly, this is how most of the financial services industry operates and is made worse when financial advisors are mainly compensated for selling products for a hefty commission and are required to hit sales quotas. A client whose money is tied up in their business is unlikely to benefit an advisor with those priorities, regardless of how much equity there may be in it.

This was the same experience that led Laura and Dale to my office.

In our first introductory meeting together, Laura explained that they were seeking to work with a CERTIFIED FINANCIAL PLANNER™ professional, as she was looking for financial advice, not financial products.

Dale also mentioned that he had heard that advisors who held that credential were supposed to be fiduciaries and were required to act in their clients' best interest, which was certainly not the experience he had had up to this point. Laura also shared that she felt she had been misled by a few other "financial advisors" she had worked with in the past who were always pitching overly complicated insurance products or investments that sounded too good to be true.

They both emphasized that the individual they would eventually hire would work with them to help assess their current financial situation and then objectively make recommendations based upon the findings.

Dale stated that he and Laura were looking to validate their current strategy and test whether they should consider other alternatives. They ultimately wanted to know if they were making the right choices with their money. Dale also mentioned that the idea of working with someone who worked with other business owners and was a Certified Exit Planning Advisor (CEPA) would be able to help advise them on their most significant asset: their digital marketing agency. Laura and Dale both mentioned that they felt their small business would ultimately be at the heart of their financial success, as their smaller retirement accounts were only being funded when they sporadically had extra cash. Even though they felt like they could easily work for another 10 years or more, Laura and Dale wanted to see all their options. This included what an outright sale of their business would look like versus possibly selling it to one (or all) of their children, should they want to take over someday. Multiple times, Dale alluded to the business's valuation they felt they had to attain to give them the freedom to quit working altogether. That was the BIG question.

The only other financial goals they gave much thought to were helping Ashley, Hannah, and Jacob pay for college tuition and expenses, budgeting for their annual family vacations, and eventually retiring together and moving closer to Laura's parents, who were currently retired and living in Scottsdale, Arizona.

Beyond that, they agreed that they had not given too much thought to the future, as the daily grind of running the digital marketing agency and raising their family took up all their extra time and energy.

By the end of our first meeting, they had defined what they were ultimately looking for: independence from having to work and having their calendars run their lives instead of the other way around.

Initially, they just wanted to feel heard and not talked down to. Nor did they want to be hard-sold.

However, once Laura and Dale chose to work with us, we went

through our financial planning process, designed to help our clients align their money with their life's values by defining what matters most to them. We then used that lens to make our initial recommendations for their initial financial plan.

By the end of our initial meetings, we had worked with Laura and Dale to discover what truly mattered most to them. Through our guided process, it turned out that they each desired a slower pace of life away from the city that they were accustomed to. They were also motivated to begin saving for and building their next home while Hannah and Jacob finished their last years of high school. After working remotely for the past year, they both realized that they could run their business from any location if they could get quality internet access. This move could finally allow Laura to build and tend to the organic vegetable garden she had always wanted. In contrast, Dale could have enough space to store his woodworking tools and have a dedicated space to work on his favorite hobby. Not to mention, all of this could be accomplished for less than they were currently paying while in their current house.

Another topic that sprouted from our initial conversations was the importance of family history to Dale. He had recently taken a DNA test online and traced his family's ancestry. In doing so, he had found a few distant family members who were still living in Ireland. He mentioned that his parents never really spoke about their Irish history or ancestors, since they were busy building their American life in the states. Dale was also secretly dreaming about someday taking a trip to Ireland to visit the land from which his ancestors had originated. After deeper discussions, we decided that we were going to plan a month-long family vacation to the British Isles for them, before all the kids were in college.

The last life goal that we uncovered together was that Laura and Dale felt like they had slowly drifted from their Catholic upbringings once their time was spent starting their business and raising a family. Laura missed attending mass with the family on Sunday mornings and the small daily rituals like praying her rosary and having family dinners on the weekend. They both wanted to re-establish those routines in their daily lives and to find a Catholic church located a few miles from the new rural home that they decided to buy only a few months after our initial discussion.

These life goals were uncovered without even mentioning their investment accounts, insurance policies, business bank accounts, or income tax rates. While we will eventually cover those topics more thoroughly, Laura and Dale felt as if they had been given permission to begin living the life they were dreaming of now before diving into the financial aspects of their situation. This motivated them to take action sooner rather than later!

Since they moved to their new home, we were also able to help them figure out how to pay for college for Hannah and Jacob— down to the penny. We worked together to determine how much financial aid each should expect given their grades, test scores, and extracurricular activities.

Both Laura and Dale stated that they did not know what they were doing the first time around with Ashley and didn't have an actual plan to pay for college. They blindly let Ashley choose the school and just dealt with their decision after the fact.

This time we helped them choose which colleges and universities were a good fit for Hannah and Jacob's respective majors and whether they were needs-based or merit-based institutions. From there, we looked at how to set aside money today that they would eventually use for eligible educational expenses in the future. We were also able to uncover additional funding options available to them as small business owners.

Just recently, we began having discussions with Laura and Dale about being more strategic regarding the valuation of the family business. In doing so, they could start preparing for its eventual sale to the kids or to a third party.

According to Dale's research, only 30% of family-owned businesses transition to the second generation, and only 12% survive to the third generation. That motivated him and Laura to begin planning early rather than waiting until it was too late and being forced to retire, like so many unprepared business owners are.

Having worked with many small businesses, a statistic that has stuck with me over the years is that when asked if having a transition strategy is important, 99% of business owners agree that it is. However, 79% of business owners have no written transition plan, 48% have done no planning whatsoever, and 94% have no written personal plan for what they will do once they sell the business and begin the next stage of life. (You can read more about the State of Owner Readiness Study at exit-planning-institute.org/state-of-owner-readiness.)

While we are still at the beginning of our financial planning relationship, I hope for thirty- or forty-plus more years with Laura and Dale. Had they not gone through our proven financial planning process, they would likely still be living in their city house, and would not have realized all the other life goals and experiences we were able to discuss and uncover together.

Laura and Dale's success is a true example of the power of real financial planning!

IN SUMMARY

- It might feel as if advisors are not willing to take on a client whose investable assets are too small to be profitable to them, but finding *real* fiduciary financial advice is worth the effort.

THE POWER
TO GRIEVE

THE EMOTIONAL JOURNEY NO ONE TALKS ABOUT AFTER THE SALE OF A BUSINESS

David Kuzma, CEPA

David Kuzma is the founder and private wealth advisor at Aquilo Private Wealth Advisors, a comprehensive financial services firm that strives to help business owners prepare and exit their business with no regrets. He is a Certified Exit Planning Advisor (CEPA) and member of the Exit Planning Institute. An Accredited Investment Fiduciary® (AIF®) through Fi360 and Certified Plan Fiduciary Advisor (CPFA) through the National Association of Plan Advisors. The author of the book, *Exit with No Regrets: A Business Owner's playbook to success before and after the exit* and has appeared in U.S. News, *Forbes* and Investopedia. He lives outside of Washington, DC, with his wife and six children. Securities offered through Registered Representatives of Cambridge Investment Research, Inc., a broker-dealer, member FINRA/SIPC. Advisory services offered through Cambridge Investment Research Advisors, Inc., a Registered Investment Adviser. Cambridge and Aquilo Private Wealth Advisors, LLC are not affiliated.

A FTER SIGNING YOUR name on the last page, a feeling of heaviness overwhelms you, but no one in the room can see it. You stand and shake hands with the three people in the room, then you leave, go back to your office down the hall and close the door behind you. You walk around your desk and sit in your chair. This feeling grows inside of you and with a blank stare, looking out of your window you ask yourself, "What the hell did I just do?"

Selling a business can be one of the most difficult and emotional experiences in one's lifetime. Even when you do everything right; building a brand, assembling an experienced team and creating a company that not only has value but reaches profitability, there are still challenges ahead to deal with after you sell your business.

If you do not prepare yourself to deal with your emotions before taking this journey through self-awareness, introspection, and exploration, it will catch up to you once the sale is final. This can lead to feelings of depression, guilt or anger mixed with regret. You will find yourself asking, "What have I done? Why did I sell my baby?"

This is the story of John, the 64-year-old owner of a mechanical engineering company. Like most entrepreneurs, John was too focused on his business to take the time to properly plan his exit. He figured he would get around to it eventually and thought he would keep working another ten years. Since John kept pushing off thinking about his exit when asked by his financial advisor, it became a critical area in his financial plan that was never addressed. Unfortunately, John soon realized he was not ready for what came next.

John started his company and grew it into one of the premier mechanical engineering companies in his community. He loved his job and considered his employees family. One day, John was approached with an unsolicited offer to buy his company for $25 million. Even though he had never thought about selling before, he realized in that moment he was getting older and wanted to spend more time with his family and grandchildren.

After taking a couple of days to think it over, John decided to sell. About two weeks later the initial terms were agreed upon and a deal was struck. It took about four months before the transaction closed. During that time, John experienced moments where he questioned himself. "What have I done? Why did I sell?" He would wake up in the middle of the night questioning why he sold when he could have easily kept growing the business for another ten years at least.

He began to realize his identity had been tied to being an entrepreneur, founder, and CEO of his company. He took great care in the responsibility of the success of his company and his employees. John also enjoyed giving back to his community through philanthropic outreach and community projects. As soon as the papers were signed transferring ownership to a corporation from Texas, a feeling of emptiness and loss began to replace what he had once enjoyed.

Weeks after the sale closed, John found his energy was drained. He barely had the desire to get out of bed in the morning. Thoughts were constantly running through his head like "I could have done this, I should have done that." He began avoiding phone calls and e-mails from friends and family checking in on him to see what he was doing with his newfound free time.

This went on for four months before John finally decided to see a therapist who specialized in helping entrepreneurs who had sold their businesses deal with the grief, loss and depression that followed. He saw improvement after six weeks of therapy, but sometimes John still longed for what used to be and wondered if selling was worth losing everything he had built.

These feelings are perfectly normal when someone sells a business. A feeling of loss accompanied by grief and depression is common for people to experience after giving up something that provided joy, purpose and identity for so long, after taking risks to build the business in the first place.

Your triggers into these feelings will be multiple and unique depending on your situation. When you lose a loved one or pet there are practical ways to deal with it, such as writing letters, creating scrapbooks or going through photo albums to address all the memories associated with them. In essence, you have time to heal because no matter how much it hurts you know they're not coming back. This is what makes selling a business so challenging—even when you prepare yourself financially, emotionally, mentally, and physically before the sale, there are still many factors that may be beyond your control.

Each of us will encounter different emotions when selling a business. No one talks about this part of the journey, nor do I know anyone who has sold their company without experiencing feelings of loss and questioning why they made the choice in the first place. There are just too many variables to account for every situation, but in being proactive before you sell, you allow yourself to experience all the stages associated with grief, which will lead to acceptance, seeing things more clearly, and knowing what you need to do moving forward.

If John had prepared himself for this emotional rollercoaster, he would have done things differently. He could have appointed a transition manager to put together action plans with milestones on how things would be handed over and who would assume those responsibilities. He might have hired a coach or therapist ahead of time to help him prepare for the emotional journey that comes with the loss of identity as an entrepreneur and leader of his business.

There are generally five stages people experience when they lose something or someone significant in their lives: denial and isolation, anger, bargaining, depression, and finally acceptance. All five stages were experienced by John, but he only recognized two for what they were: denial and depression. He was angry at himself and depressed about losing both his business and dream job. The more he thought about it the more these feelings turned into resentment towards others involved in the process, such as his attorneys, who he felt pressured him into selling even though he was having doubts.

Acceptance and finding your way forward doesn't mean you forget everything that's happened or turn a blind eye when it comes to things that could have been done differently during the sale; rather, you focus on yourself and achieving personal growth in order to move on with your life. John didn't realize this until a conversation with his financial advisor, who asked, "Well John, what do you want to do next?" It was at that moment he realized he had to do something with his life and stop living in the past.

While we can never prepare for every scenario when selling our business, taking proactive measures—such as identifying triggers ahead of time and having a plan of action to deal with each one—will help you during the transition period. This can be done by asking yourself a couple of simple questions. For example, "What in my life gives me purpose? What do I enjoy doing? Why do I enjoy doing this? Who am I outside of my business?" By approaching these questions every couple of years as an entrepreneur, you will be more prepared to define who you are after your exit.

Everyone encourages you to reach the pinnacle of the mountain and sell your business; however, most entrepreneurs are too focused on their business to think about themselves or even consider planning about what comes after they sell. Their identity can be completely wrapped in the business—more so than that of their own family. This is the main reason it is vitally important to make sure you have your own life plan outside of the business. If you are only defined by what you do for work how will you know who you are after the sale of your business?

As John recovered from his depression, I asked him why he started his business in the first place. He began to reflect on what he enjoyed the most about being the CEO and founder of the company. The more he thought about it, the more it became clear to him what was next in his life. He decided he wanted to share his experience of building a successful business from scratch, lessons learned along the way, and advice on what is needed in order to be successful when starting up your own company, so others would not have to go through the same trials and tribulations. He realized the importance of thinking ahead and preparing for life after an exit. More owners needed to prepare for the emotional journey of their exit and he wanted to share his own experience. As soon as John discovered his "why" he began making the necessary changes in his life so he could begin living each day with purpose again.

The only constant thing in our lives is change! Prepare yourself before you sell your business. By integrating a master plan that incorporates your personal, financial, and business goals you will be more emotionally prepared in making your life plan outside of the business. This way you can come out stronger on the other side!

Real financial planning is not just about the numbers in one's life, it is about helping individuals and families achieve the best for themselves. By helping prepare them for what comes next and helping them find and redefine their purpose along their life's journey.

Every hero needs a plan! You are the hero in your life's story, and as wealth managers and Certified Exit Planning Advisors we use financial planning and many other tools to help you achieve a fulfilling future. We call this "planning" because it's not just about money—but rather about creating an overall strategy for success that includes all aspects of your life. Remember, life is not just reaching the top of one mountain. It's a mountain range, and your next adventure is still to come!

IN SUMMARY

- Financial advice is not only about the numbers, but also the emotional impact when those numbers change—even when they change for the positive, as with the sale of a business.

FROM LISTENING TO ACTION: BABY STEPS TO NAVIGATING WIDOWHOOD

Todd Bessey, CFP®, MBA

Todd Bessey, CFP®, MBA is the founder of Creidim Wealth Partners, an independent financial planning and wealth management firm. His firm partners with independent women, retirees, and their families to help them accumulate, manage and conserve wealth today and for generations to come. By helping clients to avoid the noise that surrounds them, we bring focus and intention to what clients can control. Todd is also the host of the Widowed But Not Alone podcast. He is a member of several online advisor communities, including Advisors Growing as a Community, the Society of Real Financial Advisors, and ROL Advisor.

"Widowhood brought me to my knees. I may not physically show the brokenness, but my mind *is* broken."

NANCY AND I met in 2010. She had joined a LinkedIn networking group I created to help local business professionals connect in the aftermath of the financial crisis. She accepted my invitation to participate in a small group meeting over coffee. This was just a "get to know you session," and I was the facilitator. We saw each other again at some group gatherings over the next few months, but that was it.

Nancy was happily married to her husband David. Both were climbing the corporate ladder; Nancy as a benefits consultant, and David as a systems engineer for a technology firm. They were excited to be raising a young daughter and hoped to move out of their starter home after finishing some minor renovations.

In early 2014, Nancy and I crossed paths again. This time, it was under much different circumstances. Her husband, David, had died tragically several months earlier and her world was wrecked in an instant.

"When I was widowed, my world detonated," Nancy told me. "I didn't realize how bad it was going to be at the time. It was a slow rolling, thermonuclear explosion. It changed everything in my world and in my daughter's world.

"My husband died on a Tuesday, and on Wednesday morning I was getting FedEx packages from attorneys wanting me to pursue a wrongful death lawsuit. I was getting hounded. This was crazy and awful, and everything was different. I didn't know what I didn't know."

While she sat in complete mental and emotional distress, she was being asked to make difficult decisions. These were choices that could significantly impact her financial future, and she could hardly get herself out of bed. She was not ready to address these issues and took a step back from the litany of friends and family that provided opinions, made recommendations, and wanted to save the day.

A couple of months after David died, Nancy met with her accountant. He recommended she meet with me, a CERTIFIED FINANCIAL PLANNER™ practitioner, to assess her financial situation and develop a path for the future.

LISTENING

When we sat down, Nancy talked about hiring me and my firm for financial planning. I told her, over and over again, that she was not ready to make any financial decisions.

She didn't need financial advice just yet. She needed time to think and somebody to listen. You see, Nancy was still grieving. She was dissecting her marriage, her life, and her social relationships. She was trying to determine who she could trust.

We slowed the whole process down, so I could get to know her and her concerns. I wanted to hear how her daughter was doing and help with whatever she needed next.

After a few meetings, Nancy was confident that accountants, insurance agents, and financial salespeople could handle the paperwork, but she wanted to work with someone who would have her best interests in mind.

Nancy was asking me to join her inner circle of trusted advisors. She needed someone who would look at the big picture, slow it down and move at a pace that a grieving widow could handle. She wanted guidance and believed that she could tap into my network of resources.

Now, she was ready to begin, one step at a time.

BABY STEPS

At this point, I told Nancy that my role was to be there for her, to hold her hand, and to be her guide. I was there to listen, tell her the truth, and help simplify her financial life. I also wanted to help ease her anxiety, insecurity, and fear of the unknown.

We needed some time to unpack what she needed to address in the shorter term and help her answer some basic questions:

- Do I have to go back to work?
- Should we stay in this house or relocate?

- I have a small business that is failing. What next?
- How do I deal with my credit card debt, car loans, and two mortgages?
- Who will take care of my daughter if something happens to me?
- Can my daughter go to college in six years?

In the first handful of conversations, my focus was on listening to Nancy's concerns, letting her ask questions, and most importantly, allowing her to cry. We needed to have a close relationship, so that I could help her build a stable life from the one that had just imploded. My job was to provide her with the support, the information, and the guidance to move forward.

In our next meeting, we agreed to start looking at her financial resources and outline an action plan. Taking the first of many baby steps, we began assembling a personal balance sheet.

Nancy started pulling together bank and 401(k) statements, credit card accounts, car loans, the mortgage and home equity loan. When I asked about insurance, she paused and sighed. I could see tears streaming down her face. She looked up and did her best to share information about the death benefits from life insurance that were to be paid to her.

"David and I looked at each other last November and finally got serious about taking advantage of our corporate benefit packages," she said. "I told David that we needed to protect each other and our daughter, so we checked all the boxes for extra insurance."

Since David died in an accident, Nancy was entitled to the standard, the supplemental, and the accidental death benefits, which collectively amounted to a few million dollars. The death benefits paid by the life insurance company and auto insurer laid a strong financial foundation for Nancy. After we gathered the benefits and understood her financial picture better, I told Nancy that work might be optional for her going forward.

While staying at home was appealing, Nancy wanted some

normalcy and a routine, so she decided to return to work. We set aside some cash to cover the bills for the next twelve months while she considered her career options.

After gathering more details regarding her debts, we began building a plan. We developed a financial model, assessing Nancy's cash-flow needs to supplement her income. Then, we looked at assets that could be dedicated to funding retirement and the appropriate allocation to stocks and bonds. We considered paying off her loans and began to work with an attorney to help develop an estate plan.

Each step was a small victory as we checked boxes and worked our way through the comprehensive plan.

PLANS CAN CHANGE

Less than six months into Nancy's return to work, her daughter struggled to cope with the death of her father. Her grades suffered, her behavior was erratic, and depression began to set in. Nancy knew she needed to be there for her daughter, and immediately gave notice to her employer.

We began to re-evaluate her financial plan and supported her decision to stay home and figure out how to make things work.

Given that her mortgage, home equity loan, and credit cards were all at higher interest rates, we discussed paying them off versus refinancing. Nancy was a believer in the stock market and wanted to keep as much money invested as possible. But debt consolidation can be difficult without a job, as most banks require income verification as part of the loan process.

After reviewing several options with her, we agreed that the best solution was to use her bank to establish a line of credit, which was secured by part of her investment portfolio. We eliminated the other debt, and significantly reduced her interest rate and monthly payment as a result.

Now, we had to work with Nancy to establish a budget and help reign in her spending. We were feeling better about where she stood financially, and Nancy started to believe that she and her daughter would be okay.

A BIG MOVE

Just as we began to gain some stability with the budget, Nancy threw us another curve ball: Tired of home renovations and exhausted by a house that didn't feel like a home without David, Nancy needed to move. "Their" dreams were gone, and she needed to chart a new course.

She didn't want to force her daughter to change schools, so she looked for a new home in the same school district. After determining that buying wasn't the right option, we talked about renting. I advised her that this could be a wise choice, because it gave her flexibility if she decided she wanted to move again soon. We quickly found a place that was move-in ready. The old house was sold, and Nancy and her daughter moved to their new home.

At that moment, Nancy and I acknowledged that we needed to celebrate milestones like these despite the pain and the loss that was always hanging over her. She was excited to move forward, but clearly was very sad to close that chapter of her life.

With the housing situation settled, we were ready to draft an estate plan and hired attorneys at a local law firm to help. Nancy's daughter was only 13, so Nancy needed to identify someone that would act as a guardian if anything happened to her. She agonized over this decision and ultimately chose her brother.

LIFE'S JOURNEY CONTINUES

Financial planning is never a straight line. As planners, we know it's about developing a road map and adjusting as life evolves.

And just as Nancy was finding some stability in her new home, life adjusted again.

Nancy's parents were on the West Coast where she grew up. Their health was failing, and her siblings were not much help. Her mother was suffering from memory loss and her father's physical health was declining. She now had to make several trips to visit with them and advocate for them.

The emotional toll was significant, and all we could do was be there for her. When she came back to town, we met for coffee. She was exhausted and sad. She felt that more loss was coming.

She cried and then smiled at me.

"I still feel the emotions every day knowing that David is gone," Nancy said. "I also feel very blessed. We made many poor financial decisions during our marriage. But we did make a few good ones. We checked those boxes on the benefit forms. I have money, I can take care of my daughter, and I have the flexibility to leave town to care for my parents."

The most gratifying thing about financial planning is creating space for people who are struggling at the worst crossroads of their lives. Just like a marriage or birth of a child changes your life, the death of a partner changes everything. A widow emerges from that process a different person than they were before.

Widows like Nancy don't ask to be on this journey. Her life didn't unfold according to her plans. Yet, she had hope that things would change for the better, and the inner strength to live life… one step at a time.

IN SUMMARY

- Even the most complex financial challenges can be overcome if tackled a little at a time.
- Life changes as we live it, and so must our financial plans.

YOU MISSED A FEW CLASSES

Stephanie W. McCullough

Stephanie founded Sofia Financial in 2011 after 14 years as a financial advisor, with the goal of empowering women to make wise financial decisions and reduce their money stress. Financial planning plays into Stephanie's love of hearing people's stories, educating others and being a lifelong learner herself, and having a real impact on people's lives. She also frequently speaks to women's groups on topics such as the human side of money, planning for un-retirement, and financial wellness for Gen-X women. She is passionate about helping more women find and succeed on this career path.

In her free time she loves cooking, sailing, traveling, and reading mystery novels with strong female protagonists. Stephanie is married and has two nearly grown kids. She earned an MA in International Economics from the Johns Hopkins School of Advanced International Studies and a BA from Duke University. Go Blue Devils!

C ASSANDRA CERTAINLY DIDN'T want the money. She would have much preferred for her husband to still be with her. Steven—her vibrant, brilliant, caring, and funny husband—had the foresight to buy a substantial life insurance policy when their kids were very young. He couldn't have predicted his devastating diagnosis at the age of 45.

Cassandra was a health care worker. She worked with patients and their families in a hospital setting. She spoke the language of medicine and knew how to navigate the health care system. When Steven was diagnosed, it was only natural that she put on her medical hat and accompany him to appointments. As his condition worsened and he could no longer work, she became his caregiver. The family moved to a more accommodating house, and Cassandra said goodbye to her paid job.

When Steven died, Cassandra looked after her kids and worked to craft a new life for the three of them. She grieved. And she struggled with the responsibility of making all of the big decisions for her family on her own.

FACING THE FUTURE

Cassandra faced the same questions many widows do:

- Do I have enough?
- Will I be okay?
- Do I need to go back to work?
- Who can I talk to about money?

She did all the things you're "supposed to" do. She found a well-regarded local wealth management firm and asked them for help. She was with them for about a year, but she did not feel like she was a priority, so she asked around and got another recommendation. She moved her accounts to a second firm and stuck that out for a few years. But she wasn't feeling well cared for there either. When a friend from church said that her brother was a financial advisor, Cassandra thought that an individual connection would help allay her concerns. So again she moved her accounts. But that person stopped returning her calls, and instead shuttled her to a first-year staff person. Cassandra was left feeling that this must be the way the industry works: the focus is on the investments.

When I met Cassandra, she had been widowed for 10 years. She had pretty much given up hope on the "wealth management" industry. Her experience had shown her there were plenty of financial advisors willing to invest her money, but few who could help her with the other money decisions she had to make. She lived every day with worry, shame, isolation, and fear about whether she was living a sustainable lifestyle.

FINDING THE RIGHT ADVISOR

With her previous financial advisors, when she called to get cash to pay her property taxes, she was made to feel guilty for spending her own money. When she needed to help her son with living expenses, she was questioned about whether it was necessary. What she craved was someone to really talk to about the pros and cons of her charitable giving and which of her accounts she should tap for her various spending needs, now and in the future.

One day Cassandra expressed her frustration to her cousin, whom I happened to know socially. She suggested Cassandra speak with me, which she agreed to do with some skepticism.

WE TALK ABOUT ALL OF IT

I don't advise anyone on what to do with their money until I understand what they want to use it for. Money is not an end in itself: It is a tool that is supposed to perform certain jobs in our life. In order to help Cassandra address her money worries, we had to talk about *all* of it. Everything that impacts and is impacted by her money.

Here's what I learned during our first few conversations.

MONEY VERSUS FRIENDSHIP

Cassandra's best friends were from her church and her profession. They were not wealthy people. They were loving, creative, passionate, family-oriented, and very supportive of each other. And they had no idea how much money Cassandra had. She was very generous in terms of thoughtful birthday gifts and hosting meals and gatherings. But she felt that she could never discuss her money issues with them.

YOU NEVER STOP CARING AS A MOM

Cassandra's younger child, Daniel, had a significant learning disability that meant he would likely never be able to support himself. An invisible disability, it was difficult, even for people who knew him for years, to understand Daniel's challenges. Daniel lived on his own, but Cassandra helped pay his rent and expenses.

Cassandra's contemporaries largely did not have sympathy for her decision to support Daniel financially. Observing from the outside, they assumed that Daniel was taking advantage of Cassandra. Even more distressing, Cassandra's previous financial advisors recommended in no uncertain terms that she should cut Daniel off, that she couldn't afford to support him.

When I asked about Daniel's diagnosis and challenges, Cassandra admitted, "No one ever asked me before." Daniel's learning disability was tied to numbers, in that he understood math at roughly a second-grade level. Unsurprisingly, he had difficulty staying on a budget and frequently spent more than the planned amount.

DEVOTION TO CHURCH

Tithing 10% of her income was extremely important to Cassandra. It's something she and Steven had always done together, and she continued to believe in its worth. She felt it was a meaningful way to live in alignment with her values.

DUAL CITIZENSHIP DILEMMA

Cassandra had dual citizenship with the United Kingdom, so she had the option to move there someday. The upside would be a lower cost of living and free healthcare. The downside would mean leaving the community where she had lived for decades, including her friends, her church, and her professional network. She wrestled with constant doubt: If financially she needed to move at some point, shouldn't she go while she was young enough to put down new roots?

YOU MISSED A FEW CLASSES IN FINANCIAL ADVISOR SCHOOL

As is true with all clients, Cassandra's situation was multifaceted and complicated, one that was hard to appreciate just by looking at her financial numbers. After that first meeting where we really dug into Cassandra's concerns, she teased that I must have been absent the day they taught how to be condescending to clients and missed the lecture on making people feel guilty about spending their own money. When I reiterated that it is her money after all, and she shouldn't have to ask anyone's permission to use it, she took a breath and sighed with relief. "You are the first advisor to ever say that to me," she said.

What Cassandra needed from her financial advisor was much more than investment management. She realized she wanted a true decision-making partner, someone who would not judge her but would sit on her side of the table as a coach and sounding board as she worked through all the questions that touched on her money.

- The first issue we tackled was how to help Daniel understand money and his impact on the family budget. As a parent myself, I empathized with her struggle to encourage independence while still recognizing her child's limitations. Our conversations addressed our innate desire to support our kids, our worries we always carry for them, and concrete steps Cassandra could take to help her son and herself.
- We thought about the United Kingdom decision and how best to approach it. With my encouragement, Cassandra and a friend traveled to spend a few days in the town she had in mind if she had to move. They looked at neighborhoods and houses, and checked out yoga studios and churches. She gathered facts and got a feel for the area's intangibles.
- This research gave us the knowledge we needed to prepare different options in case it becomes apparent that her current living situation is not sustainable. She no longer has just Plan A: Stay where you are, and Plan B: Move to the UK. We determined Plans A, B, C and D as options to employ before emigrating across the ocean.
- As part of thinking about income and expenses, Cassandra decided to fix up her basement into a rentable apartment. Now Cassandra has a tenant who provides both income and dogsitting benefits when she visits her grandkids.
- One thing Cassandra dreaded was calling to ask for access to her money, mainly because it made her feel dependent and embarrassed. So we explored a variety of ways to forward her infusions of cash, and settled on a combination of methods. We set up an automatic monthly distribution to her bank account, a check-writing option for larger items like taxes and home maintenance, and regular friendly check-ins from our team to see how her cash flow was going.

INVESTING IS ONE SMALL PIECE
OF A FULL FINANCIAL LIFE

Today Cassandra has a much better grasp on her finances and options for the future. With steady progress, she stabilized her financial health, just as she helps improve the health of her patients. By looking at the whole person, with all of her responsibilities, aspirations, values and dreams, together we were able to align her dollars with her priorities and expectations.

As a financial planner I want to be a true partner, not someone who gives clients permission to spend their own money. My job is to be their thinking partner and accountability partner. In my work with Cassandra and other clients, I help them see the inevitable trade-offs from any financial decision so that they can come to their own, empowered decisions from a place of autonomy.

IN SUMMARY

- A financial planner is a partner who empowers a client to make decisions from a place of informed autonomy, not someone who gives (or denies) a client permission to spend their own money.

———————

The opinions voiced in this material are for general information only and are not intended to provide specific advice or recommendations for any individual security. To determine which investment(s) may be appropriate for you, consult your financial advisor prior to investing.
The views expressed in this chapter are those of the author and do not necessarily reflect the official policy or position of any other agency, organization, employer or company.

THE POWER
OF FAMILY

CONNECTED BY FAMILY MONEY

Nicola Tomlin, Chartered FCSI

Nicola Tomlin is branch principal and senior investment manager at Raymond James Investment Services Hart in Hampshire, UK. She is a Chartered Fellow of the CISI and is also a Chartered Wealth Manager. Over the 35 years that she has been looking after clients, Nicola has built a strong client base including many multi-generational families passing on wealth.

In 2018 she was invited to sit on the advisory council to the then-newly launched Raymond James UK Women in Wealth Management Network, she is keen to support and encourage diversity within the industry.

Away from finance Nicola enjoys spending time with her husband Clive and daughter Lottie, vacationing both in the UK and overseas. She is a Trustee for First Touch—the charity that supports the neonatal unit at St George's Hospital in Tooting, London.

W HERE MOST PEOPLE would sit in a chair, Susie would perch, always ready to launch into her next adventure. This was just like her grandfather Edward, it dawned on me one day.

Susie conquered mountains, literally. A semi-professional skier, she was in her early 20s, vivacious and lots of fun. She loved working the ski season in Europe, felt strongly about social causes, and was the one everyone gravitated toward at any gathering. Conversations with Susie were never dull.

There was just one challenge, and the reason I'd asked to meet with her that day. As her investment manager, I was concerned her grand lifestyle was perhaps a little *too* grand. She had a generous salary, but was spending all of it, plus regularly drawing from the principal in a trust fund her grandfather had set up for her. She'd use the top-ups to settle excess credit card bills.

When I mentioned my concerns to her, she smiled brightly and said, "I've got other trust funds."

This was true, and perhaps she'd be fine. But another thought occurred to me as she made light of her grandfather's inheritance.

She'd never personally known him.

This is how "The Letter" came to be. But first, let's take a step back into Susie's history and legacy.

THE 1900s: THAT WAS THEN

As a fourth-generation heiress, Susie was a beneficiary of wealth generated by a business conglomerate her great-grandfather had founded more than a century ago. Think Downton Abbey meets Warren Buffett's Berkshire Hathaway. She may not yet have been aware of it, but her family wealth was meant to serve as a catalyst for her own bright future, as well as a tie that would bind her to her forebears.

Susie and I represented a new era of business and wealth management—happily, one in which women are assuming important leadership roles at the generational table.

That had not been the case when Susie's great-grandfather had acquired a handful of local rental properties in the early 1900s, and expanded from there.

It had not been the case either, when his sons Edward and his brother joined the business after World War II. Thanks to the founder's prudence and his sons' hard work, business boomed. Together, they invested jointly, acquiring commercial and residential property here in the UK and overseas.

EARLY GENERATIONS: THE FAMILY TIES THAT BIND

When a third generation arrived (the Boomers, if you like!) most of them joined the business too, received a share of the inheritance, and invested it.

This was when I started working as a general administrative assistant with my father at his stockbroking firm, which meant I had the good fortune of meeting Susie's grandfather, Edward, at the beginning of my career.

What a formative relationship it was. Besides being an astute businessman, Edward had a knack for investing. He reveled in his stock picks' gains and prudently harvesting the losses for their tax advantages. Whenever he phoned us to make personal investments, other family members would almost always be in touch within hours to make the same ones.

But it was more than that. He and his brother had their eyes firmly on their family's future.

While Edward personally loved spending hours of his time studying the stock market and managing his portfolios, he knew this approach wasn't for everyone. He often told me he wanted his hard work to be there for his heirs as a safety net. If they ever fell on hard times, he wanted them to be able to go to the trust for some help.

At the same time, he told me he hoped his heirs would learn how to maintain the all-important "spend, save, invest" balance he and his brother had adhered to their entire lives.

Since Edward passed away, I have been privileged to manage the family's trusts and broader investments. Over time we have been to christenings and facilitated retirements. We've built children's and grandchildren's trust portfolios and helped them make good use of them to fund their schooling, purchase houses, and celebrate at weddings. We've walked them through the financial fall-out from divorces and sobbed together at many a funeral. When we suggest that clients often become friends or even family, it can sound cliché, but it couldn't be truer.

A LETTER THROUGH TIME

Back to Susie, in particular. With "I've got other trusts" echoing in my head, I realized that, as investment manager for her and the wider family, I was in a unique position to share more than just investment advice. I could write her a letter, to introduce her to the grandfather she'd never met.

"Dear Susie," it began. I told her what it was like for me, as a 17-year-old assistant talking to her 60-year-old grandfather. How he had patience with me when I answered the phone as a newbie. How he had encouraged me with my professional exams. How he trusted me with his trade instructions from early on, and how our relationship evolved to be more collaborative once I was more experienced. He continued to place his confidence in me as my career evolved.

I also talked about how much I appreciated some of the gentlest, open, and reflective conversations we'd had in his long life. Later in life, he had shared his aspirations with me, especially regarding the legacy he and his generation had hoped to leave. He had spoken of how hard it had been to make significant amounts of money, and how frightfully easy it had sometimes been to lose large amounts of it. He was keen to protect the family's wealth for future generations. But he also wanted his heirs to grow strong and independent, to make their own way, and to love life on their own terms.

Did the letter work? The next time we met, Susie thanked me warmly, and asked me if I could help her plan out how to better protect the assets in her grandfather's trust. "I never realized how hard he'd worked for it," she said.

An investment manager couldn't ask for a greater reward than that.

NEXT GENERATIONS: INTERESTS EXPAND AND DIVERGE

Like father, like son… like mother, like daughter? Well, to a point. When you look in from the outside, a family with generational wealth may seem like one big happy household. Take a closer look, and the view is more nuanced. Generations endure and are strengthened by their roots, but for better and worse, they also destroy, and build anew as they grow.

With respect to Susie's extended family, as the family tree grew, so too did the complexity of their relationships with one another.

On the one hand, tensions and divisions became more palpable. Each of the family units was different. Among the others, there were varying political beliefs, personal interests, and values. Some rolled with the punches, others were risk averse. Some enjoyed spending lavishly on private schools, fancy cars, and equine estates. Others were cautious savers whose children attended state-funded schools. Some were charitably inclined, others were not.

In short, despite their common heritage, each was an individual. The common thread between siblings and cousins was that they often had very little in common.

I'm happy to report Susie and I sorted out a plan based on "spend a little, save a little, invest a little" for her to fund her fulfilling lifestyle, while preserving her trust for meaningful spending. Since then, Susie has told me that she plans to share the letter with her children, nieces, and nephews when the time is right.

THINGS CHANGE

As the wider family's investment manager, my interactions with them have become considerably more challenging—as well as infinitely more interesting.

More recently, some of Susie's generation—the Gen Xers and older Millennials—have been happy to join the family company. Others needed to pursue their own interests.

So it goes. Over time, diverging interests drove the need for a family business buy-out, so each could go their desired way. Assets were sold off and proceeds split between the families. Happily, no one considered this to be a failure or a devastating event. It was clear to all, this was the beginning of a bigger evolution, and the next phase of this family's journey.

At a recent meeting with some of the family, I found that all the attendees were women, including Susie, two other advisors, and me. We agreed this would have been unheard of when the original accounts were created back in the 1960s. This too felt part of something larger, and a happy milestone for all.

As Susie and her bloodline grows, the inheritances have reduced and spread across increasing siblings. But what a treat it has been to see the fifth generation coming along, literally learning to walk on their own! The increasingly diverse, extended family is a fabulous collection of the best kind of eclectic people. And for all their differences, they are still connected to their forebears by an invisible, if enduring thread. This is the legacy their great-great-grandfather—and grandmother—began so very many years ago. Spend a little, save a little, invest a little!

IN SUMMARY

- The adage "Spend a little, save a little, invest a little" is as sound a foundation of financial advice today as it was 100 years ago.
- When planning the financials of a family (especially a large one), bear in mind that each member is an individual.

_____

A CHANGE OF (RETIREMENT) PLANS

Todd A. Bryant, CFP®, ChFC®, CLU®, AIF®

Todd Bryant is a Founding Partner and a CERTIFIED FINANCIAL PLANNER™ practitioner with Signature Wealth Partners in Orlando, FL. A Florida native, he received his undergraduate degree from UCF with extensive postgraduate studies through the American College of Financial Services. He works with business owners, pre-retirees, and retirees in planning financially for life's milestones. Todd has spent the past 15 years growing his financial planning practice from scratch through referrals, community engagement, and unique marketing strategies.

He currently sits on the UCF Alumni Board, Citrus Club Board of Governors, Outreach Love Inc. Board, and the All-Star Dads Board. In 2018, he advanced all the way to the quarterfinals of the World Championship of Public Speaking. In 2020 he was recognized as an "Honorable Knight" at the UCF College of Business Hall of Fame gala and the Orlando Business Journal's 40 Under 40. He lives in Winter Garden, FL with his wife Lindsey and two children, Cambrie and Colton.

"I F THERE'S ONE thing we weren't expecting for when we retire, it was these two blessings in disguise."

The year was 2013. Brent Weller, a prospective client for our firm along with his wife Jane, tilted his phone at me to display a pair of young boys, both about five years old.

"They sure are handsome," I said. "Are they your grandchildren?"

Brent and Jane exchanged a look.

"Yes..." Jane whispered, and paused.

"They're twins," said Brent, his eyes suddenly brimming with tears. "Trevor and Vincent."

Jane took a deep breath and continued. "Our daughter... their mom... Well, we lost her. We're raising them now."

Thus began one of the most unusual—and heartwarming—retirement planning conversations I'd ever had.

WHEN RETIREMENT PLANNING THROWS YOU CURVE BALLS

Granted, retirement can mean many different things to different people. Some imagine relaxing on a sunny beach, cold drink in hand. Others may crave high adventure, or simply relish no longer having to clock into the daily grind. Most hope to have more time and resources for spoiling their grandchildren.

But until I met the Wellers, I'd never seen a retirement plan that included starting over raising kids, all over again.

Brent and Jane had already raised their two daughters to adulthood and worked extremely hard for decades to be within easy reach of a relatively traditional early retirement, until their dreams changed in an instant. This was one reason they were seeking extra financial planning advice. Could they still fulfill some of their original goals while raising their grandkids as well? Once I got to know Brent and Jane, I concluded that if anyone could do it, it was them.

DILIGENT SAVERS FROM THE START

In some respects, Brent and Jane had been preparing for the unimaginable their entire lives. Growing up as one of six children, Brent learned about the value of the dollar at a very young age. He watched his father work four jobs to provide for his family. Jane was the daughter of Depression-era parents as well. Her father had served in World War II, after which he and his wife ran a small electronics store until he passed away in his mid-6os. There was a modest nest egg left, but Jane and her sister still had to pitch in periodically to help make ends meet for their now 92-year-old mom.

Suffice it to say, both Brent and Jane learned early on the importance of planning ahead, saving money, and not spending more than you have.

When it came to saving for their own retirement, they were ready for that as well. While Jane dedicated her energy to being a stay-home mom, Brent started putting away 6% of his income for the future. Over time, through diligent, consistent habits, they kept saving more and more every year. Brent would share with me stories of friends who didn't think the same as him. They would walk into a dealership and ask, "How much are the monthly payments for that car?" Brent's philosophy was different: "Let's find out what monthly payment we can afford, and then pick a car that fits," he'd say. Plus, he and Jane always had to concur on any major expenditures.

The Wellers routinely paid down their debts too. They strived to teach similar money management values to their two daughters.

Were Jane and Brent so frugal they never had any fun along the way? Decidedly not. Thanks to all that saving, early and often, they were able to enjoy some amazing family experiences. As the girls grew up, they took trips to Hawaii every other year. They also were able to put both of their daughters through college without incurring any debt. What an accomplishment!

However, what they didn't see coming was one of their greatest challenges, personally and financially, just around the corner.

THE MEETING

At first, before I learned about the twins, our 2013 "get to know you" meeting was relatively routine. I enjoyed hearing about their diligent, lifelong saving and spending practices. They were excited to prepare for whatever golden years they wished to have. I grew excited for them. Brent was ready to relax. He had even enrolled in a "transition to retirement" program through his employer and come up with his personal goals.

Endless golf? Coffee and paper every morning? World travels?

No, Brent wasn't one to go with stereotypes. In his plan, he wanted to work a part-time job in retirement. He wanted to move to Florida and be a Disney World boat captain. And Jane was just as excited about going along for the proverbial ride.

What an awesome goal! I have seen countless retirees get bored with the status quo quickly. Driving a boat at the "Most Magical Place on Earth" sounded like a cool way to enjoy a fulfilling retirement.

TRAGEDY STRIKES

Before I learned about Trevor and Vincent, I was assuming that becoming a Disney boat captain would be the most unique aspect of Jane and Brent's financial plans. Boy oh boy, was I wrong.

After they showed me the twins' photo, they cautiously shared with me a bit more of the story no parent should ever have to relate. Two years prior to our meeting, when the boys were only three, their mother had been killed. Clearly, she lived on in her parents' hearts, as a beautiful soul who had enjoyed music, teaching, and spending time with her babies.

Of course, the family was devastated. Brent and Jane lost a child. The boys' father was unfit to take sole custody, so Brent and Jane stepped in, just a couple years out from their "perfect" retirement. Jane commented, "Raising twins today is much more expensive than when we were bringing up our daughters in the '90s!"

THE NEW PLAN

In my eyes, Brent and Jane are true heroes. The kind you don't often get to meet in real life. If anything, the extra challenge made me want to help them all the more. After all, their unusual circumstances would call for unusual planning strategies.

Could they still retire, even if it would need to be a few years later than they initially projected? For the vast majority of families I've met over the years, the answer would probably have been "no." But for the Wellers, we were able to review some sensible scenarios in which they could possibly put themselves in that position. And, as determined as they were to do right by Trevor and Vincent, they were equally as determined to keep their retirement goals in place.

Brent was very fortunate that his company provided him with a pension. As retirement neared, we were able to walk through all the various options for taking that income. We identified the pros and cons and strategized on one of the best ways to maximize their unique situation.

Leaving a legacy behind was always something of importance to them. However, with two young boys at home, it became even more important. Fortunately, we were able to implement a plan specific to them which would ensure that the boys would be okay if something happened to Jane and Brent.

Then there was their spending plan. Brent had always read that the average retirement income need was roughly 80% of pre-retirement income. His "transition to retirement" program included a trial run. During that period, he and Jane were tasked with adjusting to a lower income while Brent worked fewer hours during the last couple years of his career. Thanks to all the saving and investing they had already completed, they were able to achieve this goal. Jane had long been the household bookkeeper (as well as a professional one, once their daughters had grown), and kept a close eye on the family budget.

A DISNEY ADVENTURE

Believe it or not, after some interim consulting work, the family moved to Florida, and Brent actually did secure that dream retirement job as a Disney Boat Captain! I was excited to hear the stories and fascinating memories he and Jane collected from that period.

After more time had passed, Brent decided he'd "sowed his wild oats" and could hang up the ole captain's hat. To me, this illustrates another advantage of ongoing planning. Brent took the part-time dream gig, knowing the income would be nice, but not essential to their success. As Jane explained, "We decided we'd rather take the kids to Disney than be working there."

These days, the Wellers have moved back to the mountains, to enjoy the beautiful scenery as the boys have entered their freshman year of high school. This also puts them closer to their other daughter and her family. Once the Wellers reach age 72, they'll need to start taking taxable required minimum distributions (RMDs) out of their tax-sheltered accounts based on current tax law (which is subject to change). In their situation, they were able to utilize converting from pre-tax to after-tax dollars which could potentially save them tax dollars in the future.

In the meantime, Brent is a substitute teacher at the boys' school, while Jane enjoys her hard-won leisure time. Brent is not teaching because he *needs* to for extra income, but because he *wants* to spend even more quality time with his grandsons.

Again, while it's been a privilege to help the Wellers navigate their retirement years, a huge benefit has been the phenomenal saving they've stuck with throughout their lives. I'd like to think the extra planning eased their financial decision-making during challenging times, enabled them to still spend their retirement years the way they wanted to, and even facilitated a couple trips to Disney World, where Brent was able to relax, and not worry about driving the boat.

IN SUMMARY

- Saving early and often can soften the financial blows of even the most devastating and life-altering challenges.

THE BLIND SPOT OF LONGEVITY

Amar Pandit, CFA

Amar Pandit is a CFA Charterholder from CFA Institute, Virginia, and is a CERTIFIED FINANCIAL PLANNER™ professional. He is also an alumnus of the Wharton School of the University of Pennsylvania.

Amar is the Founder of Happyness Factory, a world-class, planning-focused, goal-based online investing platform through which he aims to help every family save and invest wisely.

He is also the Founder of HappyRich Capital, which helps families live the lives they have imagined with their money (a HappyRich Life).

He is very passionate about spreading financial literacy and does so through his sharp and analytical posts published regularly on www.happyrichinvestor.com and www.happyrichadvisor.com.

He is the author of five bestselling books, eight sketch books and over 1200 columns for various newspapers and publications such as *The Economic Times*, *Mint*, and *The Indian Express*.

He lives in Mumbai with his wife Laxmi, two daughters (Reet and Preet), parents (Nalini and Prabhakar) and their pet, Fudge.

To RETIRE AT 45 (or at an early age) is a fantasy that many individuals cherish. There are even several movements such as FIRE (Financial Independence, Retire Early) and FatFIRE that talk about retiring early all the time.

IT TRULY SOUNDS LIKE THE DREAM, DOESN'T IT?

Peter, a Corporate Executive in his early 50s, had been dreaming about this for the last 10 years. He was diligent with his savings and investments but had never figured out how much was "enough" for him to retire in the next five years.

I met Peter through a friend of mine. We had set up a meeting to figure out not only how much was enough, but also to figure if there were any blind spots in the planning that he had done.

Peter was a savvy finance guy, and besides some number crunching, he had made the following interesting observations.

- I want to maintain my current lifestyle as long as I live.
- I want to invest in my personal education and growth (I plan to attend an advanced management program in an Ivy League school).
- I want to support my family.
- I want to be able to pay for my family's medical expenses.
- I want to leave money for my daughters.
- Additionally, I want to support causes that are important to me.

As we were discussing his observations, I asked him, "What's keeping you up at night?"

"It's not that I don't understand money and finance," Peter said, "but the key thing that keeps me up at night is that I might be missing something. I am sure there are some blind spots. So I want a financial advisor to give me a view and a detailed plan of action on the following things:

- Is there something that I am missing (blind spots)?
- Do I have enough?
- Am I on track?
- If not, what do I need to get back on track?
- Will my family be okay if something happens to me tomorrow?"

CHANCE I WILL SEE A BLIND SPOT

WITH FEEDBACK

ON MY OWN

BEHAVIOR GAP

After patiently listening to Peter, I asked him this question: "What's important to you about money?"

Though it's a difficult question for most people to answer (if you don't believe me, try answering it!), Peter was quick to respond: "Security and lifestyle."

I prodded him further: "What's important about security to you?"

He responded by saying, "I want to make sure that my family is taken care of in my presence as well as in my absence."

"What's important about that, Peter?" I asked with a smile.

He was starting to see the pattern... and starting to really open up.

He said, "Well, that is what I live for, Amar—my family. They are the most important people in my life."

While there were no tears here, I could see that his eyes lit up every time he spoke about his family. He was a complete family man—a loving grandson, son, father and husband.

We spoke of his early childhood, his family, and many stories around growing up in New Jersey.

At the time Peter still lived in Monroe, New Jersey with his wife Anne and daughters Liv and Elizabeth. Peter's mother Margaret and father John, who was in his mid-70s, lived close by, together with Peter's grandfather, 98-year-old Tim.

During our conversation, I figured out that his grandfather Tim had been needing regular financial support from his father John for almost a decade. At the same time, Tim was reasonably healthy and likely to need financial support for at least a few more years, in addition to any health emergencies or health situations that might arise.

Supporting Tim had put strain on John and Margaret's—not to mention Peter's—finances. Peter knew that he might have to step in to support all of them at some point in the near future.

While Peter had been saving, investing, and planning diligently, he hadn't factored in how his family's longevity could affect those plans.

WHAT DO I MEAN BY "LONGEVITY?"

In simple words, people are likely to live longer than they used to. In fact, they already do. Look at some of the people around you, or at your near and dear ones. We are all seeing people living into their nineties and some who have even crossed 100.

We are living in an era with amazing advances in medical treatments and technology. Gene editing is one such technology that will likely change the way diseases are treated. Don't just believe this. Read a fascinating book by Walter Isaacson called *The Code Breaker: Jennifer Doudna, Gene Editing, and the Future of the Human Race*, to understand the progress in medical science and the impact this could have on our lives and longevity.

Even without gene editing, people are living into their late nineties and early hundreds. What do you think would happen *with* gene editing?

What are the personal finance implications for the person living to 100? That could be 35–40 years after retirement! It wasn't that long ago that life expectancy was about the same, or even lower, than what we now consider standard retirement age.

Peter realized that this was his biggest blind spot. It was a true "Aha!" moment for him. He realized that his father was likely to live well into his nineties, and Peter was hoping for the same for himself. There was no number crunching or any talk about the financial markets. We were purely having a conversation about Peter's financial life and how it interacted with and supported what was truly important to him.

His first important question seemed like it was answered.

The three expensive questions then for him were:

1. How much is enough considering the longevity that runs in my family?
2. Am I on track to address this?
3. What do I need to do to ensure that we never run out of money?

Peter was confident he had enough. But when we started to crunch the numbers, including financial support for his father, we realized Peter would outlive his money by his mid-70s if he were to start supporting his father or grandfather for just eight years.

Peter realized that his retirement plan was myopic on the longevity aspect and the impact this longevity (that ran in his family) had on his personal financial goals.

Besides renaming his *retirement plan* as a *longevity plan*, we factored in support for John for a couple of decades while even considering any support that Tim would require. We figured out Peter's number for "How much is enough?" so he would never have to worry about money for his lifestyle, or that of his parents.

Just addressing this blind spot of longevity and getting this initial part of planning right gave Peter the clarity that he was always looking for.

We also reworked what was truly required for his other financial goals.

We came up with a list of specific action points and decided to check in regularly for the first 12 months, and then once every six months from the second year onwards.

Peter took up some consulting gigs and increased his savings substantially. He changed his asset allocation from a very conservative one with loads of debt to one that was skewed towards equity, with a sizeable chunk of his portfolio in cash for any contingencies that might come up. This was also called his "peace of mind" portfolio, one that would help him weather any correction or crash in the stock market.

He invested regularly (including some of the inheritance his wife Anne received), and rebalanced not too frequently, letting his gains compound.

His daughters, Liv and Elizabeth, now study in the New England area and Peter has funded their education as planned. He is now supporting John, who is now in his early eighties. Tim passed away at the age of 101. There are several other milestones coming ahead for Peter (who's now 56), but he has planned well and he is on track not to outlive his money.

IN SUMMARY

- Increased life expectancy, not only of us but also of our elderly dependents, means that we need to change our assumptions about financing retirement.

THE POWER OF
INDEPENDENCE

BE CAREFUL WHO YOU TRUST

Cathy Curtis, CFP®

Cathy Curtis, CFP® is the founder and CEO of Curtis Financial Planning, a full-service financial planning firm based in the San Francisco Bay Area serving clients nationwide. Cathy's mission is to be a fiduciary financial partner for independent women, so they can feel confident about their finances while pursuing what they love and do best. As a CERTIFIED FINANCIAL PLANNER™ practitioner and member of CNBC's Financial Advisor Council, Cathy is a frequently sought-after author and contributor. For more than a decade, she's shared her unique financial planning insights via her award-winning blog, Of Independent Means, and widely followed Twitter feed (@CathyCurtis). In 2020, Cathy launched the Financial Finesse podcast to showcase successful, interesting women and provide actionable advice for her listeners. For the last seven years, Cathy has been named an Investopedia 100 Top Financial Advisor. Investment News also recognized Cathy as one of its 2020 Women to Watch for her contributions to the profession and financial literacy, and support of women inside and outside the industry.

"**I** FEEL SO FOOLISH,"" Tamara said as she nervously fidgeted in her seat. "I can't believe he duped us like that."

Tamara, a widow in her early 40s, looked distraught as she shuffled through the papers she had brought with her that morning. Her mother, Rose—a petite woman with a kind face—reached over and grabbed Tamara's hand. "It's okay, dear," she said. "We're going to get this fixed."

DOOMSDAY

Tamara had called me a week prior expressing anxiety about her financial situation. Her husband, the breadwinner of the family, had passed away suddenly earlier that year. Overnight, Tamara became a widow, single mother of two teenage girls, and head of the household finances.

Seeing how overwhelmed Tamara was, Rose encouraged her to contact her cousin Ron, an investment advisor. Ron had managed Rose's money for several years, and Rose thought working with him might take some pressure off Tamara.

Tamara took her mother's advice and contacted her cousin. Now, six months later, Tamara was becoming increasingly concerned with how he managed her and Rose's money. While she didn't know much about the stock market or investing, Tamara had a bad feeling about the investments Ron had made on their behalf—her account values had started to fluctuate wildly over the last few months. She wanted a second opinion and found my website after a late night of Googling.

Tamara was thorough in her due diligence. She scheduled two separate phone calls and asked for references before agreeing to meet with me. This time, she wanted to take full ownership of finding an advisor she could trust to have her best interests in mind at all times. I'm sure she wanted to get some stability in this part of her life too, and I assured her that I would partner with her to help her reach that goal.

A NEW PERSPECTIVE

I looked at Tamara and Rose, sitting opposite me in my office. "Tamara," I said, "This isn't your fault. You made what you thought was the best decision for your family at the time. Why don't we go through the account information you brought with you?"

Tamara began spreading papers across the table. As I looked at her account holdings, I realized her instincts were correct. Ron had put her and Rose in some incredibly risky investments—investments that would be inappropriate for even the most seasoned investors. I couldn't believe it. The majority of the portfolio was invested in inverse and leveraged exchange-traded funds (leveraged ETFs attempt to amplify returns of an underlying index by using financial derivatives and debt, while inverse ETFs are a bet on the underlying index going down— otherwise known as a short strategy). He also had their funds invested in commodity stocks, real estate and oil and gas partnerships—all investments that can be highly volatile.

Rose began to speak softly. "Tamara said she was worried about Ron, so I asked my sister Ann, Ron's mother, about it. Ann told me that Ron had been following the investment advice of a popular doomsday prophet who writes an investment newsletter. Apparently, he was investing all his clients based on this person's recommendations. But she said she was too embarrassed to tell me. I wonder how many other people don't know."

"Okay," I said. "You were right to seek another opinion. The good news is that these investments are liquid and we can sell them and reinvest your funds."

Over the next few weeks, I worked with Tamara and Rose to reinvest their accounts. In this case, I knew it was imperative to get them out of the risky investments that Ron sold them and invest their money more prudently. So I sold the assets Ron had purchased and invested their accounts in a more diverse and risk-appropriate mix of funds. I documented the new investment strategy in an investment policy statement, which they agreed upon and signed.

This wasn't the first time that I had worked with a woman who relied on a relative to help her invest her money. Many times, fathers help daughters or brothers help sisters. Women have been known to lack confidence when it comes to investing compared to their male counterparts, so gladly delegate the task. I feel strongly that a woman needs to be intimately involved with her money matters and to resist the urge to rely on someone else. Even when working with a professional advisor, it's important for a woman to be involved in all key decisions.

PROGRESS STALLS

Just as I was about to get started with the financial planning process with Tamara, progress stalled. Tamara was so relieved to have gotten her investments stabilized that she dragged her feet on getting me the information I needed to start a plan.

I realized that I needed to be flexible. Tamara was dealing with a lot in her personal life. Her two daughters were in their early teens, and one of them suffered from social anxiety, so Tamara needed to provide her with extra encouragement and support. In addition, Rose was beginning to show signs of senility. Tamara knew that soon Rose would have to move from the family home into a care facility.

At the same time, Tamara was attempting to turn her part-time technical writing position into a full-time role. Because she was preoccupied with resume-writing and networking, Tamara couldn't find the time for long-term financial planning.

A MODIFIED APPROACH

Tamara's situation was one that I often see with women clients. Women are usually the caretakers and have competing priorities, making life frantic and exhausting. She is also part of the "sandwich generation," which refers to middle-aged people caught between caring for both children and parents emotionally, physically, and financially. So I knew that I didn't need to add to her stress by pushing her to complete a comprehensive plan on my timeline.

Instead, I decided to take a modified approach and tackle each component of a comprehensive plan one at a time, based on importance to Tamara's particular circumstances. So, we started with insurance, the bedrock of any financial plan. Since I don't sell insurance myself, I referred Tamara to a few insurance professionals I trusted to keep my clients' best interests at heart.

Together, we made sure she had enough life, liability, disability and long-term care insurance to protect her from life's risks.

Next, we tackled estate planning. Tamara's husband hadn't been thorough in his estate plans, leaving her with a mess to clean up after his death. She didn't want her children to have to deal with the same thing. She and I discussed her wishes for distributing her assets after her death and who she would appoint as her representatives. Then, she felt prepared to work with an estate planning attorney to draw up all necessary documents to complete her estate plan.

Just as Tamara was thorough in her search for a financial advisor, she conducted the same level of due diligence in hiring an estate attorney for herself. She felt it was important that she find someone who was a good listener, empathetic, and also technically competent. She found an excellent attorney who I now refer to other clients.

MOVING FORWARD

Tamara was glad to get these pieces of her financial puzzle resolved. Over the following months, we tackled more aspects of her financial plan until it was complete, things such as cash-flow planning, expense planning, and charitable giving strategies. With these major decisions behind her, Tamara felt free to focus on the rest of her life, including her new career path.

Today, Tamara is well on her way to reaching her goals of raising thriving children, making sure her mom is comfortable and cared for, and enjoying a stimulating career. She landed a full-time job as a technical writer and now is making and saving more money. With Tamara's help, Rose moved into an assisted living facility. In addition, we set up college savings plans for both of her daughters, and she set up automated contributions out of her paycheck.

I caught up with Tamara during a recent client review and asked how she felt, now that more than a year had passed since our initial meeting. She told me she had so many sleepless nights right after her husband died—and working with Ron didn't help. But, now that she had a plan and a solid investment strategy, she felt like a huge weight had been lifted. For the first time, she was excited to blaze a new trail for herself. She couldn't wait to see what comes next.

IN SUMMARY

- It can be risky to rely on well-meaning family to guide your investment portfolio.
- Even when working with a professional advisor, it's important for a woman to be involved in all key decisions.

GOLDEN YEARS

Jessica L. Fahrenholz, CFP®

Jessica Fahrenholz, CFP® is a financial planner and investment adviser at Tudor Financial, a registered investment advisory firm in Dayton, Ohio. She is passionate about helping her clients make sense of their financial circumstances and giving them the education and confidence to make sound financial decisions. In addition to the AGC, Jessica is a member of the Financial Planning Association (FPA) and CFP Board.

Securities Offered Through Westminster Financial Securities, Inc.

Member FINRA/SIPC.

"**H**ELLO, JESSICA?"

I'd picked up right away when I saw the caller ID display: *Jim Parks*. Jim was not yet a client, but his parents, Dave and Clara, were.

"Um, Mom and Dad are down at the car dealership. They just tried to buy a car."

Ordinarily, buying a car wouldn't require an emergency phone call. Even if it did, I wouldn't ordinarily be legally (or ethically!) permitted to speak to a client's son about it.

But this was no ordinary call.

A SATISFYING RETIREMENT

Let's roll this story back to the summer of 2015 when I first met Dave, a World War II veteran, and Clara, a retired teacher.

At the time, Dave and Clara were in their late 80s, living their golden years in a retirement community near Dayton, Ohio. They were healthy, active, and happy. Clara was religious about her daily walks around the facility. Dave spent his time on the golf course and in the woodworking shop where he made toys for underprivileged children.

After nearly 70 years of marriage, they were also still madly in love with each other. Over the next five years, my business partner and I had the privilege of working closely with this delightful couple. To know them was to love them, and throughout our time together, they would share more about their lives and their love story.

INDEPENDENT MINDS

Throughout their lives, Dave and Clara had essentially been financial "do it yourselfers." Even without the help of a professional, they made many responsible decisions throughout their lives. They lived well within their means, invested consistently, and held their portfolio steady across stock market ebbs and flows. By doing so, they'd accumulated a substantial nest egg to provide financial security in retirement.

So, why did they come to us?

In 2015, Dave's memory was beginning to decline. Wisely, their tax preparer recommended they meet with a financial planner.

HOW CAN WE HELP?

We first met with Dave and Clara to listen to their concerns and find out how we could best help. Their biggest concern was how they would manage their finances—which Dave had been primarily responsible for until now—as they faced Dave's health problems. Clara was worried she wasn't up to the task.

Together, we roughed out a plan to simplify, well, everything. Dave and Clara needed guidance in several areas, including:

RECORD-KEEPING AND ORGANIZATION

Dave and Clara had decades' worth of paperwork filed away. They kept everything, not knowing what was important to keep or what they could throw away. Their investment portfolio included many accounts, which compounded the difficulty of keeping track of everything. Time spent going through piles of paperwork in their home ultimately uncovered additional investment accounts they had forgotten about.

INVESTMENTS

Dave was a savvy investor who consistently contributed to their investments over many years. With our help, Dave and Clara could make some changes to better align their portfolio with their needs. For example, delegating the ongoing supervision and management of their portfolio allowed Dave and Clara to reduce risk, diversify their holdings and introduce more tax-efficient investment vehicles. Perhaps most importantly, we could reduce some of Clara's angst around managing their finances. We could also improve the record-keeping problem by consolidating their accounts to a more manageable number.

TAXES

Taxes kept Dave up at night. Even with the help of a trusted tax professional, Dave constantly worried about their tax situation throughout the year. They had been making quarterly estimated tax payments, and they always worried about whether they had remembered to send the checks in on time. So instead, we suggested we increase withholdings on their retirement distributions and retirement income sources to take those fears away.

A FINANCIAL MANAGEMENT JOURNAL IS BORN

Due to Dave and Clara's age and health concerns, we felt it was important their family be comfortable with the idea of us working with their parents. Family dynamics can be complicated, and it's generally best to have transparent conversations when the situation allows.

Here's another tip we shared with Dave and Clara, which we would recommend for any family facing dementia: We put together a *financial management journal*. Like a diary or an eye-witness account to your household wealth, your journal can summarize conversations you've had about all things financial. Dave and Clara's journal had notes from our meetings, investment statements, and reports. It included copies of signed paperwork and items we were working on, like reviewing their estate plan and arrangements for final wishes. This is helpful for any family as months turn into years. It becomes a must-have if dementia strikes.

PRECIOUS MOMENTS

Journal aside, we talked a lot with Dave and Clara as we checked in with them monthly. Each visit, they'd greet us at the door with the same excitement you'd imagine your own parents or grandparents having.

Dave had fought in the Battle of the Bulge, and he would occasionally share stories about those times. Mostly, though, he and Clara talked about their life together. Their love for one another was contagious, with evidence of it everywhere. Clara would leave poems for Dave to find near his computer. At nearly every meeting we had, Dave would interrupt our conversations, look at his wife, and exclaim, "Isn't she just beautiful?"

Clara would tease Dave about how she'd played hard to get with him in high school, even though he'd been the big man on campus, with several sports scholarships to his name. Then she'd laugh and remind Dave (in front of us), "It worked, didn't it?"

MEMORIES FADE

As time passed, Clara began having her own memory issues, sometimes worse than Dave's. Some months, Clara would look at the pages in their financial management journal in confusion. Then, she would look to us and ask if they really did have that much money.

Dave would also tell us he couldn't sleep at night, worrying whether they had enough money for Christmas presents or if they would run out of money altogether. Even though they had amassed a large safety net, they could scarcely believe their journal was accurate, as their minds took them back to earlier times.

THE CAR SITUATION, PART 1

Roughly two years later, Clara and Dave faced a new challenge. As they were out driving near their home, they looked around and realized they were lost. The two spotted a police officer and asked for directions back home. When they couldn't come up with the name of their retirement community, the officer was concerned. This situation caused the retirement facility to revoke their car privileges. This was necessary for their safety and the safety of others, but imagine how devastating it was for a strong couple like Clara and Dave to lose the independence a car represents.

THE NEXT GENERATION WEIGHS IN

Around this time, we met with Dave and Clara's son Jim for the first time. Understandably, he was apprehensive for and protective of his parents—

which is where that now two-inch-thick financial management journal came in handy. Given their declining health, Dave and Clara agreed to grant Jim a power of attorney, so he could take a more active role in managing their daily finances. This also allowed us to share information more routinely with him. For all concerned, Dave and Clara's financial management journal gave us a big head-start as trusted relationships and family roles began to shift.

THE CAR SITUATION, PART 2

In the meantime, Dave and Clara remained upset over "the car situation." They just weren't willing to give it up. Every meeting, we would tell them they had plenty of money to hire a driver and that their retirement community provided transportation options. Neither of these was acceptable to this determined pair.

Which returns us to that phone call I received from Jim. Dave no longer had his license at this point, and we never figured out how they could nearly make a new car purchase. Luckily, Jim was able to stop the transaction before the deal closed.

But that wasn't the end of it. Another afternoon, Jim called again. It was July and roughly 90 degrees out when Dave and Clara attempted a two-mile walk to a nearby store along a busy rural road. Their plan? To purchase two bicycles. Luckily, that same police officer from earlier was driving by and recognized them, giving them a safe ride home.

Their last attempt was during a meeting with us. Dave looked at me across the table and offered to give me all their money if I would help them get a new car in return.

He meant it.

This was a sobering moment for me as an advisor. Dave and Clara were strong and independent but also vulnerable.

GOLDEN YEARS AND
A FAMILY LEGACY

We continued to serve Dave and Clara until their final days. As financial planners, we were able to act as their financial "quarterback," working closely with other trusted professionals and their son, Jim, making sure Dave and Clara's financial needs were met.

Despite facing the scary realization of dementia years earlier, Dave and Clara took control of their lives by implementing a financial plan. This allowed them to live their golden years with a sense of direction and purpose, ultimately leaving behind a legacy for their family.

Working with Dave and Clara was truly an honor, and I only wish we had met them sooner. To this day, I use cooking utensils in the kitchen that Dave made in the woodworking shop and regularly talk with Jim and his wife, who are now clients.

IN SUMMARY

- Family dynamics can be complicated, and it's generally best to have transparent conversations when the situation allows.
- Keeping a journal of financial management activities can build trust and give peace of mind not only to clients, but to their entire family.

PLANNING FOR DISABILITY

Matthew G. Ricks, MBA, CFP®

I'm Matt—the founder of Haystack Financial Planning, a registered investment advisory firm in New York. As a financial planner who serves the disabled community, I have found a way to merge financial planning with my passion for serving others. I am a CERTIFIED FINANCIAL PLANNER™ professional that operates on a fee-only basis.

I currently live on Long Island with my wife and our two sons. We enjoy pretending to be dinosaurs, shooting hoops, and having silly dance parties. When not spending time with my family or running Haystack, you may find me walking one of the local golf courses, tapping a beat with my fingers (I'm a recovering drummer), searching for the perfect grilled cheese, or contemplating my next home improvement project.

"IF SOMETHING WERE to happen to you, she could lose her benefits." When those words registered with Stacey (insert the *Dragnet* voiceover about how names were changed to protect the innocent) her shock was palpable over Zoom. We were 15 minutes into our second meeting and reviewing her accounts. She had multiple investment accounts with her daughter Sarah listed as a joint owner. Typically that's not a big issue and usually only has FAFSA or Kiddie Tax implications. The difference, in this case, is that Sarah is autistic.

Allow me to take a step back and set the stage by providing more information on Stacey and her situation.

The genesis for our discussion was that she had recently accepted a severance package for her job as an executive at a well-known sweets company. Stacey was in her mid-50s with two children, a 23-year-old son who was out of the house living on his own and a 16-year-old daughter, the aforementioned Sarah, who was living with her. She had been through a tumultuous divorce a few years before and was finally feeling like she was "back on track." In her mind, she was only 7–10 years from retirement and was looking for help on what to do next.

When reviewing your finances, it helps to make a list of the "positives" and "opportunities." For most of us, this will be the first time all of our finances are listed in one place. It also can help shift perspective from the minutia to the proverbial big picture.

Overall, there were many "positives" for Stacey. She was extremely diligent with tracking her monthly expenses and had her budget laid out in a categorized and color-coded spreadsheet. She had over $750,000 in her 401(k) and was maxing out her annual contribution. There was over $1.5m in her taxable investment accounts. There were term life insurance policies with death benefits of $500,000 and a whole life insurance policy with a $300,000 death benefit plus $20,000 in cash value. Her estate planning documents (will, medical directives, etc.) were up to date. Other than a mortgage, she had minimal debt.

Now let's take a look at the other side of the ledger.

The most obvious "opportunity" was a lack of income. She worried as an older woman (her words not mine) at her salary level it would be difficult for her to get a role at another company within the industry. Leaving her job meant losing her health insurance and enrolling in COBRA for benefits. This also probably meant an increase in out-of-pocket medical costs. She bought her house in late 2018 when mortgage rates were at their most recent peak.

Those weren't even the trickiest aspects of Stacey's financials. She had the ever-stressful situation of mingling family and money. Her brother owed $45,000 from a loan when he hit a rough patch a while back. She was also helping support her aging father.

Now let's explore how Stacey and Sarah got to this point.

During Stacey's divorce, she wanted to update her estate documents. Her attorney helped set up a special needs trust (SNT) for Sarah and suggested opening an ABLE account—both excellent ideas. They also recommended Sarah not be listed as a beneficiary (primary or contingent) on Stacey's 401(k). Another smart move. The investment accounts were opened post-divorce and thus not part of the attorney's review. Stacey opened them under joint ownership based on the advice of her previous financial advisor.

Why are the investment accounts in joint ownership with Sarah an issue? Well, it has to do with Sarah's eligibility when she applies for Supplemental Security Income (SSI) or Social Security Disability Income (SSDI). These programs are dependent on an applicant's assets and income. For the sake of time, we'll only focus on SSI.

The first requirement for SSI eligibility is that you must be 65 or older, blind, or disabled. The Social Security Administration (SSA) determines someone under the age of 18 be disabled if they "have a medically determinable physical or mental impairment (including an emotional or learning problem) that results in marked and severe functional limitations and can be expected to result in death or has lasted or can be expected to last for a continuous period of not less than 12 months." Since Sarah meets the SSA definition of "disabled" we can stop there. Nope, the second aspect of SSI eligibility is where the fun begins.

A number of the requirements were not an issue for Sarah. Out of the remaining six, the two most relevant for Stacey and Sarah were limited resources and limited income.

The SSI limit for resources is \$2,000 for an individual. The definition of "resource" includes cash, bank accounts, stocks, and life insurance. Remember how the attorney recommended removing Sarah as a beneficiary on Stacey's 401(k)? If Sarah were to inherit that money directly, it could be considered an available resource. Also, had Sarah retained joint ownership of the \$1.5 million in the investment accounts, the SSA could determine she had \$750,000 available to pay for her care. Well over the SSI limit.

Sarah also has an ABLE account. For SSI purposes, the first \$100,000 of an ABLE account balance does not count towards the resource limit. The balance was around \$40,000 so going forward, if we kept the balance below the threshold, these funds would not negatively impact Sarah's SSI benefit. Stacey would also be able to continue adding to the account each year to help pay for Sarah's care.

Generally, the more countable income you have, the less your SSI benefit will be. Income is broken down into three main categories: earned income, unearned income, and in-kind income. Here's the catch though: Some of your income may not count as income for SSI. Again for the sake of time, we won't get into what counts and doesn't count. Simply know that if your countable income is greater than the allowable limit (\$794 per month for an individual in 2021), you cannot receive SSI benefits.

Seeing as Sarah was not working yet, earned income was not currently an issue. However, the other two were very prevalent. Part of in-kind income is food and/or shelter received for free or less than fair market value. Unearned income includes interest and dividends. The investment accounts were earmarked for Stacey's retirement and it's likely at some point they would contain dividend-paying stocks or coupon payments from interest-paying bonds. Sarah's SSI benefit calculation would include part of those amounts if she were to continue being listed as an owner on the accounts. Some of you may be asking, "Why couldn't you simply change the investments in the accounts?" Adjusting the investment mix to qualify Sarah for SSI benefits would cause them to be misaligned with their main purpose: Stacey's retirement. Sarah's future care was no doubt extremely important to Stacey, but having those accounts available for her retirement was more of a priority.

If all that wasn't confusing enough, the SSA can also count a portion of the income or resources of a spouse, parent, or parent's spouse towards an applicant. They refer to these as "deemed income" or "deemed resources." These could both apply to Sarah as a disabled child under age 18 living with her parent. Waiting until after Sarah turns 18 to apply for benefits would eliminate the "deemed income" possibility.

Another thing to be conscious of is that giving away a resource to get below the SSI resource limit could lead to being ineligible for SSI for up to 36 months. If we waited to make the change until Sarah was 18 and had already applied for SSI benefits, there's a chance the change in account titles could be viewed as her "giving it away" so she could be below the resource limit.

Now that you're thoroughly versed in SSI eligibility, it's time to discuss how we addressed the outstanding issues for Stacey and Sarah.

During our conversations, the possibility of Stacey doing freelance consulting kept coming up. Throughout her career, she built up a robust network and had the needed contacts. This would also provide the freedom for her to spend more time with Sarah and potentially travel more often. She really took to the idea after spending her entire career being an employee, with all the expectations that go along with that. We worked with an attorney to get an LLC established, and within a few weeks she had her first few contracts.

Being a freelance consultant had its downside when it came to health insurance. Stacey's COBRA benefits only lasted for 18 months and afterward she would have to rely on the Marketplace for coverage. We adjusted her budget to include significant increases in her premium costs until she reached age 65 and applied for Medicare Parts A, B, and D.

We got a bit of good news as we were going through the financial planning process. Stacey's brother had sold his house and would soon have the money to pay her back. We worked out two repayments with $20,000 coming after his buyers paid the initial deposit and the remaining $25,000 after the sale closed. The first payment provided Stacey with the cash needed to cover a few months of expenses while also not causing another cash-flow crunch for her brother.

Working with a mortgage contact of mine, we were able to refinance Stacey's mortgage and reduce her interest rate by more than 1%. We also changed it from a 10-year adjustable-rate mortgage (ARM) to a 30-year fixed rate. Some financial planners would disagree with extending her obligation by 20 years when she wanted to retire in the next 7–10 years. For Stacey, it was about certainty. Shifting from an ARM to a fixed rate meant she knew what the exact amount would be for the foreseeable future versus a possible increase if interest rates rose.

We decided Sarah would not apply for SSI benefits until after she turned 18 to eliminate the possibility of "deemed income." That would also give us ample time to change the titling on the investment accounts and avoid it being seen as Sarah giving away the resource to be below the resource limit.

The next thing was to change the titling on the investment accounts from joint ownership to Stacey individually. This kept the accounts aligned with their main purpose, Stacey's retirement, and meant that when Stacey did pass away they would go through the probate process. Any funds left in the accounts would then be distributed according to Stacey's will. In this case, Sarah's inheritance was funneled to her special needs trust which in turn would fund the ABLE account, being sure to keep the balance below the $100,000 SSI threshold.

Even though the documents were only a few years old, we did a full review of Stacey's estate plan. Doing so we discovered that a guardian was not named for Sarah. Why was this important when she was 16 years old and would be considered an adult in a couple of years? It's because once Sarah turned 18, establishing guardianship if something were to happen to Stacey would become a much more arduous task. By having this already in place, we were trying to ensure the continuity of Sarah's care.

The Center for Disease Control (CDC) estimates that one in four adults are living in the U.S. with some type of disability. That's approximately 61 million people who need assistance navigating the various government benefit programs, private benefit options, and more on top of their existing finances. I like to think Stacey's previous advisor meant no harm with their suggestion to open the accounts in joint ownership and that it was simply a matter of them being unaware. There lies one of the biggest issues faced within the financial advice profession.

This was one of the first financial plans I worked on that involved helping those with disabilities. There was a lot I didn't know, which led to a lot of research and time spent trying to find resources. I also didn't know it at the time, but it started me on the path to focusing on the disabled and special needs community. This experience eventually led me to launch my firm, Haystack Financial Planning, dedicated to serving that community.

IN SUMMARY

- One in four adults in the U.S. are living with some type of disability, and might need assistance navigating the various government benefit programs, private benefit options, and more on top of their existing finances.

LIVING YOUR OWN
FINANCIAL LIFE

Kevin Mahoney, CFP®

Kevin Mahoney, CFP® is the founder and CEO of Illumint, an award-winning Washington, DC-based company that specializes in financial planning for Millennials. Kevin focuses, in particular, on empowering Millennial parents to invest in their family's future. His non-judgmental, empathetic financial planning process helps his peers save for college, repay student loans, buy a home, and learn to invest. Business Insider recently named Kevin one of the "best financial advisors for Millennials" in the U.S., and his two young boys recently named him "best father in the world."

I T WAS THOSE voices again.

That was the best way to describe the feeling. Even if you would never state publicly that you were hearing voices in your head.

Not loud exactly, but persistent. Like an unremarkable pop song that stays with you far too long after the music actually stops playing. For Josh, it was his dad's soft-spoken baritone. For Amanda, her mom's self-assured, but cautious, intonation.

Those voices were not real in the way that a child hears a parent command, "Time for bed!" But they had real power, all the same.

And Josh and Amanda had, at last, reached an impasse. They needed to confront those voices.

JOSH AND AMANDA HART

Josh and Amanda Hart don't think of themselves as particularly unique. "Two young kids, a house… yadda, yadda, yadda," you might hear them say. Translated, they mean that they're young enough to fear the move to the suburbs. Old enough, though, that they don't feel particularly enthused to be at a bar after 11 pm. Their starter home couldn't possibly be a forever home. But a forever home feels like it might take—well, forever—to get. Their paychecks are high by any reasonable standard. Yet, like any good Millennials, they still feel a twinge of guilt with every latte they buy. Even more stressful: the idea of wealth, which feels as foreign to them as their recent promotion to soccer parents. Still, they're fortunate, comfortable, and generally happy.

On some level, their status quo suits them. Why disrupt a not-so-bad thing, right? Except, they can't shake a constant, underlying feeling of anxiety. Sure, part of it may just be FOMO. But there's more to it. Their parents' voices—their parents' experiences with money—currently hamper their ability to live their own financial lives. They don't feel empowered, don't feel free, to make confident financial decisions. They feel stuck. They feel paralyzed by the unavoidable financial trade-offs that most of us face. And they fear what will happen if they don't do something about it.

TRAPPED IN THEIR FINANCIAL PAST

By all accounts, both Josh and Amanda's parents are lovely people. They care dearly for their children, a fact best reflected in how hard they worked to provide for Josh and Amanda growing up. Still, they didn't make much money. And they would concede that finances periodically caused tension at home. But their love and effort ultimately gave Josh and Amanda the opportunity to live better lives when they became adults themselves.

Perhaps it was somewhat inevitable, then, that Josh and Amanda's married life would look much different than what their parents experienced as young adults. Josh and Amanda don't live in the same part of the country, don't work in the same industries, don't use the same modes of transportation, don't spend their free time in the same places. Up until recently, though, they have shared at least one thing: how they think and feel about money.

Josh's first memory of money dates to the year that he desperately needed the hottest basketball shoes on the market. To him, an impressionable pre-teen focused only on his social standing, they seemed attainable enough. All of his teammates showed up to practice that winter wearing a pair. But in private, the response from mom and dad was, "Too much, Josh."

Amanda, meanwhile, recalls the year one of her closest friends invited her on a vacation with her family. "I have a place to stay!" Amanda pleaded with her parents. She just needed them to pay for her airfare. "Maybe when you're older," they told her. "When you have a summer job, and you've saved up."

Over time, the luster of those shoes, and that trip, faded. But those feelings —shame, guilt, embarrassment—are a different story. They, too, *seemed* to fade. After all, they didn't bubble up on a regular basis in the years after. And they didn't damage their relationships with their parents.

But as Josh and Amanda began to manage their own finances, those same feelings lurked like a ghost. Neither Josh nor Amanda recognized them initially. They couldn't put a name to the feelings, nor fully grasp their impact. But they loomed almost as if their parents were doling out the same disappointing advice in real time.

In their 20s, those voices created nothing more than a minor, irritating feeling of uncertainty; a buzzing fly amid relatively inconsequential financial decisions. But as 30-somethings, Josh and Amanda felt like they faced an endless supply of daunting financial choices. Those voices, as always, reverberated through their minds unchecked. And they were becoming more and more incongruous with their adult identities, resources, and opportunities. The stakes had increased.

CHOOSING ACTION, EVEN IN THE DARK

Amanda still remembers the night that the lightbulb came on. It wasn't much more than a flicker; not exactly the bright white light you might, for example, shield your eyes from in a dentist's office. Even so, it was enough to illuminate an initial path forward.

Josh and Amanda were lounging on the couch after finishing their takeout, simultaneously watching TV and scrolling through their phones. Josh asked Amanda if she had seen the latest *U.S. News* college rankings, which had come out earlier that day (their alma mater had jumped up two spots). Almost immediately, Amanda's mind redirected her to anxiety about college savings—more specifically, the lack of college savings they currently had. Josh and Amanda had been meaning to invest in a college savings account roughly since the day their oldest son, Noah, had arrived four years ago. But, for some reason—many reasons, in reality—it hadn't happened yet.

At first, they were too tired. Then, they procrastinated. Later, they were busy. Most recently, they had hesitated. Their progress (if you can call it that) usually stalled when thoughts such as, "What if..." and, "But..." entered their minds. They wondered whether they should save more for their own retirement. They worried that they should keep extra cash for an unexpected emergency. And they questioned whether they shouldn't just try to pay off their own student loan debt once and for all.

In short, they feared a mistake. They dwelled on the possibility that they might make the wrong decision. So on all of the days before this one, inaction felt like a better choice than action.

This day turned out differently, though. While Josh rattled off a list of colleges they dreamed about their kids attending, Amanda quietly pulled up Google and typed in "financial advisor Washington DC." In hindsight, she had no idea what she was looking for or what she expected to find. But she was pleasantly surprised by what she saw. Or, perhaps more accurately, what she didn't see.

Most of the search results didn't point her to someone 30 years older than her; she saw that several financial advisors around her own age offered financial planning. Most of the websites didn't prominently display retirees walking down a beach (as those NFL ads seem to do each Sunday); she saw that a few financial advisors specialized in the specific decisions she cared about. And most of the sites didn't ask her and Josh to find about $600,000 in additional wealth to qualify for help; she saw that some financial advisors focused on actual financial planning, not just an investment portfolio.

Less than 15 minutes after Josh had raised the subject of college, Amanda announced, "I think we should meet with a financial advisor. Take a look at the links I just sent you." And that's how they found me.

A PLAN FOR THE PERSON
(NOT THE MONEY)

Timid smiles greeted me the first time Josh and Amanda Hart's faces popped up on my Zoom screen. Warm smiles. Optimistic smiles. But smiles that nonetheless said, "We're not quite sure what we've gotten ourselves into."

The first thing I said to them was unremarkable, at least on the surface: "What's on your minds?" Amanda took a noticeably deep breath, then let it out in a long exhalation. An exhalation suggesting that, for the first time in her life, she might be able to relax when thinking about her money. No one had ever given her space to ask her most personal financial questions out loud. No one had ever shown a willingness to listen to her financial worries. And she certainly had never felt comfortable sharing her financial concerns so publicly.

Josh, when he first spoke, was best described as eager. Eager like a track runner who jumps off the starting blocks before the gun goes off. Josh's self-doubts manifested themselves in a different way than Amanda's—he wanted to talk specifics. He was ready for me to give him actionable tactics. Technical terms like "mutual funds", "average returns", and "interest rates" all sprang from his mouth within the first few minutes of our conversation.

Neither Josh nor Amanda's approach to financial planning was right, or better than the other's. They were venting, in their own unique ways. They were expressing what felt most critical to them at that particular moment. Amanda's underlying uncertainty needed acknowledgment, needed validation. Josh's more visible nervousness, meanwhile, reflected a need to do something today. Anything to feel productive, to make up for lost time. Yet, they already had made meaningful progress.

From my perspective, I wanted to understand more about who they were as individuals, as a couple. I wanted to get a sense for how happy they were with their lives. And I wanted to try to tease out what they wanted from life in the future. In theory, I was in a position to immediately give them exactly what they thought they reached out for: a clear, detailed college savings strategy. But a few months, maybe a year, later, they probably would have felt financial uncertainty again. The strategy probably would have fallen apart. If we didn't address the true, underlying reasons they needed guidance, the financial plan would have failed.

Josh and Amanda's detailed college savings strategy, then, began from a much higher altitude. In our first few meetings, we talked about what decisions they might make if they had unlimited resources. We talked about what decisions they might make if they only had a short time to live. And we revisited their experiences with money growing up. Such conversations may sound like couples therapy, rather than financial planning. But these discussions reveal what people value. They shed light on what money means to them. And the information that emerges is what actually makes a financial plan work over the long term.

FROM TALK TO TANGIBLE CHANGE

After our second meeting about these questions, Josh said, "This was great, thank you." But I hadn't actually given him and Amanda any specific financial recommendations yet. What I had given them was new ways to think about the role money plays in their lives. I had prompted very personal discussions that they had never considered. And now they needed to turn their insights into tangible change. Here's where I suggested they start:

SPENDING AND BUDGETING

Josh and Amanda are frugal enough that they don't need to cut back on spending. But they would benefit from tracking their expenses more carefully each month. Ultimately, we want them to learn how to spend more money, without stress or guilt, on the purchases that make their lives great.

EMERGENCY SAVINGS

The couple probably could put much of their savings to more productive use elsewhere. Even so, for them, a larger emergency savings account aligns with how they think about risk and security. I encouraged them to view this as an example of a situation in which the math on paper doesn't always prevail.

STUDENT LOANS

Josh and Amanda could refinance their federal student loans to a lower interest rate. And they could pay off the balance more aggressively. But they have other, most important priorities right now. By holding on to the benefits that federal loans provide, they can buy the flexibility to pursue other things in life.

RETIREMENT

Retirement isn't all sunsets and sailboats for Josh and Amanda's parents. Their kids have noticed, which has sparked in them a greater interest in their own retirement savings. But as long as they place a higher value on college, I asked them to give themselves the permission to take a more incremental approach to retirement contributions for now.

COLLEGE SAVINGS

Josh and Amanda recognized that even their highest financial priority doesn't come without potential drawbacks. To combat the unknowns about what college may look like for their kids, I voted that they invest for college through both education and other types of accounts. College may be the target today, but this approach provides space for that intention to change.

Would Josh and Amanda actually take these steps? We had aligned their financial plan with who they are, but they now had to understand the role that timing would play in the outcome.

THE CLOCK STARTS TICKING

Money isn't a particularly fun topic for most people. So it's a bit paradoxical to describe a young couple as excited about a financial plan. Yet, there we were! Josh and Amanda described their new financial path as "freeing."

They sensed they could finally shed much of the anxiety that had dogged them over the past few years. But a very real possibility still existed that Josh and Amanda would not follow that new financial path.

After all, planning is not the same as doing. Josh and Amanda felt encouraged, motivated in this moment. But nothing about their demanding work schedules had changed. Nothing about Noah's and his brother, Oliver's, temper tantrums or restless nights had changed. Wedding seasons would still hit their calendars hard, as would extended-family gatherings and highly encouraged work happy hours. If they didn't start empowering themselves to shed their parents' voices, they truly might miss out on valuable financial opportunities.

A MONEY SCRIPT IN THEIR OWN VOICE

Uncertainty defines almost the entire college savings experience. Yet, this isn't the uncertainty that had proven to trip up Josh and Amanda through Noah's first four years. Rather, they needed to confront the overall financial uncertainty that their own life experiences had generated. Their financial circumstances no longer looked the same as their parents', or their teenage selves'. They knew this on some level, but they didn't know how to recalibrate their decision-making.

The financial plan that Josh, Amanda, and I ultimately created gave them the specific steps to create the lives they want for themselves and their kids. But that's not what empowered them to succeed. They changed their financial lives by countering those voices in their heads with a script of their own making. Those voices will never quite leave, but their power had changed. Josh and Amanda had redefined what roles they should—and would—play in their own financial lives.

IN SUMMARY

- When people reveal what money means to them, the information that emerges is what actually makes a financial plan work over the long term.

———————

THE POWER
TO GIVE

LIVING TODAY, PLANNING FOR TOMORROW

Elliott Appel, CFP®, CLU®, RLP®

Elliott Appel, CFP®, CLU®, RLP® is a fee-only financial planner. He is the founder of Kindness Financial Planning LLC, which focuses on helping widows, caregivers, and people affected by major health events gain control of their financial life. In addition to writing regularly about financial planning strategies, aging issues, and caregiving, Elliott hosts a podcast called Making the Most of Time. He has been quoted in *The Wall Street Journal*, *Associated Press*, and many other publications. Elliott is a member of the National Association of Personal Financial Advisors (NAPFA) and XY Planning Network. He currently lives in Madison, Wisconsin to support his wife's career in medicine, but calls the Pacific Northwest home.

L EO WAS GOING to die. We didn't know when, but a few of us in the room were confident it would be in the next few years.

As I sat across from Leo and Sara, I had a hard time "keeping it together." In other words, I wanted to cry.

Leo was diagnosed with stage four lung cancer, the same exact disease my dad had been diagnosed with a year prior. The average life expectancy is about six months.

Although I had not been married for nearly 60 years, I knew some of Sara's pain. I knew the pain of uncertainty. I knew the constant battle between hope and sadness. I knew the routine of endless medical appointments.

I could see it in their eyes, even though their journey with the disease had just started.

They set the meeting because of his diagnosis. Leo had always managed the household finances, which included stewarding their investments, preparing their tax return, and paying the bills. Like most families, they divided labor.

THE FIRST MEETING

During our first meeting, I knew something special was happening. Not only was I ready to work with Leo on understanding his system, honoring what he had built, and creating new plans with them to make it easier when he passed, I had a good understanding of what they might experience on their cancer journey. After all, Leo was about to start his first round of immunotherapy, and he was going to take the same drug my dad was taking.

The first step we took together was understanding where they were today and where they saw life headed—not only now, but after Leo passed. It's impossible to map out, but we needed to discuss what they wanted life to look like with the time they had remaining together.

Sara was sharp. She read the company literature closely, picking it over with a fine-toothed comb. Unfortunately, there is a real distrust—and rightfully so—of the financial services community. The barrier to entry is low, and people are commonly taken advantage of. Sara and Leo were following a thorough vetting process, which is exactly what I would have done.

After we had answered her questions, we talked about the specifics of what Sara and Leo's financial future might require.

During one of our first few meetings, Sara said, "I plan on Leo being around for a long time. I don't want to look at the spreadsheet he built when he is not here in three years." I understood. The reality was that he probably wouldn't be here in three years; however, like with my dad, I hoped he would be.

DO YOU HAVE ANY GRANDPARENTS?

As the meetings progressed, Sara asked, "Do you have any grandparents?"

I said, "No, my grandmother passed away while I was in high school, and she was the only grandparent I ever knew."

With a warm smile and an inviting look, Sara asked, "We already have grandkids, but could we adopt you?"

Here we were, a few meetings into the relationship, and they were ready to become my adopted grandparents. Those are the types of couple—those who on the heels of their 60th wedding anniversary already have a beautiful family, but make room for others—who you want to have more time together.

From the outside looking in, many people believe financial advising is a one-way street. The advisor advises the client. The truth is that most advisors learn just as much, if not more, from their clients. They learn how to be better human beings, show more compassion, avoid mistakes in life, offer forgiveness when wronged, and all the other messy life lessons people take a lifetime to experience. We get to see these qualities unfold in the relationships we develop, and if we are lucky, allow them to impact our own lives.

MAKING CHANGES AFTER 60 YEARS

Sara and Leo impacted my life from the start.

In those initial discussions, we focused on their financial independence plan to show that to remain financially independent, they did not need to take as much risk. Leo historically had their investments allocated to 70% stocks and 30% bonds, mostly in active mutual funds.

Although Sara was not involved in the day-to-day decision-making, she acknowledged we would be a big change for Leo. We were suggesting changes after 60 years of doing it one way.

After talking it through, we agreed on a shift to reduce the risk in the portfolio. They did not need as much risk, and having a little more security was prudent given they did not know how their housing situation might change as Leo's health worsened.

With an investment plan in place, we started working on other items that would make it easier when Leo passed away. Like most people, Leo had his passwords written down on a few pieces of paper. Although many people see a financial advisor as only helping with finances, everything impacts finances in some way. Because of this, very few topics are off-limits, including helping with password management systems.

THE GIFT OF ORGANIZATION AND SIMPLICITY

Unlike most people, Leo gave Sara an incredible gift. He outlined where their accounts were located, who to call when he got sicker, important professionals in their life, why certain accounts existed, and any other small details Sara would want to know about their financial life. It's something I am recommending to anybody in a similar situation going forward.

It was up to all of us to simplify this as much as possible.

The first task was creating a better system for managing their passwords. Instead of writing everything on a piece of paper, which sometimes, but not always, was updated when passwords were changed, I talked to them about a password manager. I explained they only needed to remember one complex password, which would let them into a system that would manage their other passwords.

The change did not happen immediately, but over time they worked on converting from their paper system to the password manager.

Check, one thing simplified.

Next, we discussed their charitable giving. They gave regularly to charities, often supporting more than 10 charities per year. The problem was that Sara had never done their taxes, and I shuddered at the thought of tracking 10 or more donations per year.

We talked about a donor advised fund because I wanted them to give as tax-efficiently as possible and avoid tracking multiple donations. This strategy provided them with a simpler way to donate investments that went up in value, take a larger deduction in the current year, and allow them to support the charities they had already been supporting over time. Their charitable giving now had a more cohesive, simplified plan.

WHERE TO LIVE—HEALTH DECLINING

As with anything in life, there are not answers for every problem. They had set their life up around walking. They lived close to a grocery store, theater, music, and anything else they wanted to do. As Leo became sicker and had vascular issues, walking was tough. While a 10-block walk in the past would have been normal, making it a few blocks was painful and tiring.

We started initial conversations about other living situations. Did a continuing care retirement community make sense? Should they buy into something now? Should they sell their condo to lock in the gains from a lucrative real estate market?

You can build nearly perfect spreadsheets and analyze the

numbers to your heart's content, but finances are wildly emotional. And rightfully so. In this case Sara was not ready to move from the apartment, and they could arrange for care if needed. They decided the condo was still the best choice for them, but it was important to talk through the options and determine how each would work financially.

LAUGHING, SMILING, AND PREPARING FOR LOSS

Throughout our meetings, Leo would worry about various investments. When emerging markets were doing poorly, he wondered whether they should have exposure to them. When Brexit happened, he was worried about the recovery time in the portfolio.

One of my favorite moments was after a few minutes of Leo talking, Sara nonchalantly stated, "Leo, don't you always say 'ride it out and be patient'?"

I paused, chuckled a bit, and said, "I couldn't have said it better myself."

Leo responded by laughing and admitting that is what he would say. We all had a good laugh that day. Leo had one of those laughs that could infect a room. He projected a warm, inviting kindness with it that drew in even the shyest of people.

We started talking about tax planning and their estate plan. They knew they wanted to update their estate plan, but like most people, they felt paralyzed by it. They had done it, but something prevented them from signing it.

I offered to review it with them. Making it a priority was important because Leo's health was up and down. Although the immunotherapy had been effective at first, one of the tumors had grown. He also had blood transfusions and was experiencing aphasia, a condition in which it is difficult to express oneself. It often shows up with a loss of common words. Leo would tell a story and get stuck on a word everybody at the table knew, but he couldn't find it. I was familiar and empathetic to it because I saw how it affected my dad in his disease. We took the time to go through their estate plan, page by page. We confirmed that important people were included for the right roles, discussed the tax benefits included in the plan, and what it would look like to handle the accounts when Leo passed. They signed it shortly after our discussion.

LEO'S PASSING AND THE SURPRISE GIFT

Leo's diagnosis changed their retirement plans and shortened their time together, which in turn changed their tax planning and how they made gifts to kids and grandkids.

We made it through the big planning items. Their finances were simplified. We had systems in place for Sara to take over some aspects and hired professionals in the other areas. It's nice when a plan is developed from the start and slowly chipped away at until it is accomplished.

I knew Leo almost two years before he passed. It was sudden, and yet it wasn't. That's the way cancer goes. It's expected, but it's not. There always feels like there should be more time.

I went to Sara's a couple of weeks after Leo passed. She shared what had happened. I listened. We cried together.

That's the strange thing about financial planning. It's *felt*. It's *experienced*. I can tell someone what I will do, but until we go through it together—to really experience it—they will never know.

It's amazing the little ways Leo popped up after he passed. Almost two years later, Sara was participating in a virtual tea tasting with me during the pandemic, and suddenly, she dropped off the call. That was very unlike her to abruptly leave.

Later, I found out that her computer battery was dying, and when she went to get the charger she found it "secured to the wall so well it wouldn't move in an earthquake."

Who had done that?

Leo.

IN SUMMARY

- Although many people see a financial advisor as only helping with finances, everything impacts finances in some way.

SAVE A LIFE?

Shanna Due, AFC®

Shanna Due is an Accredited Financial Counselor (AFC®), co-founder of The Due Collaborative consulting group and Due Financial.

Whether working with her financial planning clients, consulting through The Due Collaborative, or volunteering in support of her local community and military families, Shanna is committed to seeing individuals use their capital, time, treasure, and talents to create a life focused on making an impact in the world around them. She has served as a board member, an advisor, seminar leader, and coach to hundreds of participants ranging from teens to retirees.

Shanna currently lives in Williamsburg, Virginia with her husband, two children, and rescue pup. In her free time, you can find her on the sidelines cheering on her children, searching for a hidden mountain lake, or reading a book on her latest obsession.

"WE WOULDN'T HAVE to wait," Brody whispered to his partner, who quietly reached for his hand and gripped it tight.

A simple statement. But I could see the revelation hanging in thin air—ephemeral, and yet shimmering so bright and clear, it would take but one more breath to make it real.

SAVING AND SPENDING

Brody and Vince came to me several years ago with big plans for their life together, along with big saving imperatives if they wanted to make those plans happen.

First, they wanted to marry, and celebrate that milestone in style. In their late 30s, they couldn't count on parental contributions to fund their wedded bliss, so they knew they would need to save for that on their own.

They also had grand visions of their dream home. Both longed to move out of their urban apartment into a "real" house, with a yard and a patio where they could entertain friends and loved ones. As they dreamed about those days, they bantered about how many rooms they would need, and where they would ideally locate the grill and smoker they did not yet own.

Of course, later down the line, they'd want to retire. Children? Probably. Well, maybe.

So far, their saving goals had been relatively typical. But their next statement took me by surprise.

"We want to save a life."

I don't remember my exact reply, but it went something like this: "Ok… tell me more."

I couldn't wait to hear about it.

IN SEARCH OF SOMETHING MORE

When I met Brody and Vince, they'd already been together for seven years. Brody was a licensed therapist working as a case manager at a major medical institution, where most of his clientele were families facing life-altering situations. He found the work rewarding, but with 12 years of tenure, he had reached his income potential. Vince was a project manager for a non-profit organization. He also enjoyed his work. Plus, he had opportunities for growth.

In short, while both had productive careers, they also wished to do more to contribute to a better world.

That's where their idea about "saving a life" came in. But what did that mean? Even they weren't entirely sure.

BRIGHT LIGHTS, BIG CITIES

At first, they talked about whether having children would fulfill their life-saving goal. They considered various parenting options, but ultimately decided none felt like the right path or optimal solution for them.

We kept digging. I learned they both had volunteered with an organization that helps refugees settle into communities. They considered "adopting" a refugee family and supporting them with a monthly stipend. It was a cause they felt strongly about, but it still didn't quite click.

Setting the subject aside, we continued to talk about their wedding, home ownership, and retirement plans. As we did, each began to describe what they'd learned from watching their grandparents and parents make their way in life.

That's when things got personal.

Brody had grown up in a rural farming community, where his neighbors and family were intolerant of him being a gay teen, and then a gay man. It had been both liberating and terrifying when he'd moved to a large city, leaving open wounds behind him. He'd found a supportive new world in the city, but he was also overwhelmed by its complexities. At the same time, he struggled—and largely succeeded—at forgiving those he loved.

As he spoke, Vince was nodding knowingly. While he had not been ostracized by his adoptive parents, he had always felt like they believed he was in some sort of phase he'd grow out of. When he too moved to the big city, all alone, it was both exciting and enormous.

No wonder they both brightened as they spoke of the volunteer hours they'd spent helping homeless teens, most of whom had been disowned by their families after identifying as LGBTQIA+. In unison, they began to mention ways they wished they could do more, if they only had more time and money to give.

"Well, what if you *did* have more time and money to give?" I asked.

Because sometimes (and admittedly, these are often my favorite times) we financial planners get to play devil's advocate.

A LIFE PROJECT TAKES SHAPE

As we talked it through, what began as a mirage soon transformed into a tangible thing, which we then referred to as their "life project."

They were planning to get married, but hadn't yet set a date. They had set an approximate budget, but weren't sure if it was reasonable. (It helped that Vince was also a trained chef, and Brody loved his creations.) Having watched their grandparents and parents age, both felt strongly about making sure they were prepared for retirement, especially in a world where they only had each other to depend on. The house, too, required some calculations to find the right balance between excessive and "enough."

All these wants and needs required coming up with specific dollar amounts, as well as discussions on how to prioritize the inevitable trade-offs. I lean toward prioritizing financial goals by those that have the greatest consequences if they're not met. This doesn't work for every financial planning scenario, but in this situation, Brody and Vince agreed.

They quickly determined having enough for retirement was the most important. Then what? What if we could shift some of their assumptions, and carve out more time and money for their life project?

As a licensed therapist with a specific expertise, Brody had once mentioned in passing that he might transition into a part-time private practice as he approached retirement.

I challenged him: "What if you didn't wait until retirement to do that? Would that work for you financially?"

We worked through the numbers. We decided, if Brody went into private practice right away, he would have to work full-time for the first year. But in subsequent years, he could likely reduce his hours and maintain his current salary. Especially if they decreased their wedding budget by a bit, they could keep their retirement contributions the same *and* keep saving for a house, if a slightly more modest one.

With each decision made, their life project came into sharper focus. Brody would have more flexible time as a private therapist. And by freeing up more cash flow through a few other acceptable budget cuts, they could direct some of their time and money to offer transitional housing for teens who were aging out of foster care. As a loving couple (one of whom is a therapist), Brody and Vince could be there to support, mentor, and empathize with these young adults as they matured.

THE POWER OF PLANNING

Today, Brody and Vince are happily married, looking to close on their new home next spring, and have been spending more time and money helping teens and young adults navigate the city without familial support.

It all began the day they realized they wouldn't have to wait until they retired to make their life project a reality. We can't know if they've actually saved a life, or how many. But I think it's safe to say they are making an important difference today, without sacrificing their own future to do so.

Sometimes, all it takes is for us to imagine, *"What if?"* for a better world to come into view.

IN SUMMARY

- Sometimes, all it takes is for us to imagine, *"What if?"* for a better world to come into view.

THE POWER
TO RECEIVE

FROM UNANSWERED QUESTIONS TO FINANCIAL CONFIDENCE

Melissa Joy, CFP®, CDFA®

Melissa Joy, CFP®, CDFA has worked in the investment and financial planning world for more than 20 years. In 2018, she founded a new wealth management company, Pearl Planning, located in Dexter, Michigan. At Pearl Planning, Melissa and her colleagues like to say they offer clients "financial planning for real life."

Melissa works with clients at all stages of life. Particular areas of focus include life transitions, such as divorce and widowhood, as well as planning for entrepreneurs and those receiving equity compensation. Outside of work, Melissa loves spending time with her husband, Jeff, and school-age children, Gus and Josie.

WHY? HOW? WHAT *should I have done differently?* When a loved one dies by suicide, these are the questions we ask. We ask, knowing there are no answers. At least none that offer any solace.

When even the most critical queries fail to fill the vacuum, how can financial planning help a surviving spouse?

Let me tell you the story of my friends Elizabeth and Steve. One of the bravest people I know, Elizabeth has permitted me to share her journey, along with her memories of her husband. Stitched together as snippets in time, their tale informs us about the power of financial planning to weave strength and resilience in times of grief.

BEFORE: ON THE PLAYING FIELD

Elizabeth and I met more than a decade ago through our community soccer league. Before that, she and Steve had met in the same way, through the same league. We were all in our early 30s. Happy, healthy, nothing particularly heroic about us.

Our acquaintance soon deepened into friendship when Elizabeth and I both became league board members. Together, we tackled a few organizational challenges, with Steve and my husband cheering us on. Eventually, we began to spend time together beyond the field. One of our earliest gatherings stands out in particular: Steve and Elizabeth had bid indulgently at a silent auction fundraiser for a local food pantry, and won a private dining experience for four, donated by an up-and-coming (now renowned) chef.

I will always remember what it was like to be a guest in their home for such a special occasion. I remember the friends who offered to watch our toddler son that night. I remember Elizabeth and Steve's welcoming kitchen. I remember the heavenly courses "our" personal chef prepared.

I remember, because the evening was unforgettable.

BLACK FRIDAY

Several years later came another day I'll never forget. It was the day after Thanksgiving. Even our son was sleeping in, so I missed the first few times my phone rang. When it rang again and I answered, it was our minister Tiffany, a fellow soccer teammate and friend. She was calling to tell us Steve had died during the night. There was no need to whisper, but she did so anyway: "Suicide."

What?!

"Stunned" hardly captures it. How could this be? Steve was quiet and earnest. From all appearances, he was a devoted husband, and a kind man, well-regarded by friends. He was an intelligent hard worker in a promising career. He loved foodie experiences and exploring new places. If he had inner demons, he never shared the extent of his pain. Not even with Elizabeth, who was understandably in shock on that dark, dark day.

TRIAGE IN THE AFTERMATH

When tragedy happens, everyone wants to help. But how? Well-intentioned family or friends may attempt to take over and make things "better." There's an understandable impulse to make decisions on behalf of a widow or someone else experiencing the pain and vulnerability of an unfathomable loss.

I hate that loss of agency. In the aftermath of a tragedy, most decisions can wait. I say this as a financial planner, and as a friend.

In the first few days, the biggest help was spending the night with Elizabeth, acting as a buffer between her and the void. We sat in dark rooms where it was safe to express grief and anger. We did little else. I was one of many friends and family on call ready to help.

Gradually, time returned. After a few days, there were tense moments trying to retrieve passwords from Steve's computer. Quiet words were spoken: "Are you okay with money and bills this week?" "When you need to make a call, I can get who you need on the line." "If you have questions, I can help you find someone to provide answers." Most of all... "Remember, you don't have to take care of it now."

Those are the words I think worked best, until she was ready to take a few breaths.

A few weeks after the funeral, Elizabeth asked me to help her sort through some of Steve's accounts in more detail. This was the beginning of a bridge from my being her friend, to being her friend plus financial planner. I know some financial planners are reluctant to work with friends. I happen to think differently. If you find me in a room of friends, I won't be trying to pitch my services. But if someone I know asks me to work with them, I often say yes. In Elizabeth's case, I'm glad she asked.

CLAWING OUT: THE INDIGNITY OF "I'M SORRYS"

Even in the best of times, it's difficult to understand how a list of accounts, a pile of investments, and cash in reserve translates into knowing you have enough. What are adequate funds for a lifetime? Especially for those who are newly widowed, retired, divorcing, or otherwise undergoing a big transition, I've found I can best illustrate the answer to, "Am I okay?" by beginning with the basics, and layering in the intricacies over time. The first time you crunch the numbers is not enough.

Elizabeth and I started looking at her financial circumstances in chunks of time. Early conversations focused on the immediate future: "You just need to get through these urgent things now," I told her. "Soon, we'll tackle the important questions about how you'll be over time."

Then there were the equally daunting personal challenges. How many times should a new widow have to explain to a random stranger on a customer service line that her 30-something husband has senselessly died? When the agent on the line talks about his "retirement," it feels so wrong. (Can't you see he never *got* to retire?) From collecting on life insurance, to retitling retirement accounts, to notifying Social Security, and more... we navigated through the infuriating phone menus and interminable holds ("Your call is very important to us… *not!*") to sort through the aftermath, and explain the circumstances over and over again.

Through all this, we had to have long conversations to affirm this was money that was Elizabeth's. Her funds were not "Steve's money" or "blood money." That perception and perspective couldn't be updated with a phone call or new account form. The world seemed unfair, and the humiliation intolerable. Institutions simply aren't built for the task. As we helped Elizabeth settle Steve's estate and establish her own "Am I okay?" financial affairs, I hope we helped assuage the pain and indignity at least a little bit.

STARTING OVER AGAIN: PERMISSION FOR SELF-CARE

Even as time presses on, grief has no calendar. Wounds remain raw. Ongoing self-care remains a priority, as does essential financial planning to cover the costs.

So it went for Elizabeth. In the days after Steve's death, as well as years later, critical self-help questions continued: "Can I afford to take some time off?" "Can I afford to work part-time for a while?" Elizabeth and I sorted through these and similar questions over time.

Whether it's during a crisis or "just because," I encourage being as generous as you can when nurturing your mental health. I like to build deep, personal engagements with my clients, but I can only take it so far. The same can be said for friends and family. Sometimes, only a professional therapist will do. I often work with families to make space for this essential expense by budgeting it straight into their expense column. They can then permit themselves to spend generously on self-care when called for.

ELIZABETH MAKES HER MOVES

Over the years, Elizabeth and I have revisited her numbers time and again as her questions and opportunities have evolved—sometimes for better, sometimes for worse. Financial planning software provides the quantitative answers, but our conversations have filled in the qualitative gaps.

One of our first planning projects offered Elizabeth the confidence to sell the house she and Steve had called home. She took some time to travel and explore. She then moved across the country to the San Francisco Bay area, and took on a new job.

Time passed, Elizabeth put down some roots, and we revisited her plans. With continued self-care in mind, she upsized her Bay Area apartment to a roomier unit in a better neighborhood. The extra space was nice, but there was another reason for the upgrade....

Elizabeth and Steve had never had children or pets, but Elizabeth had often dreamed of adopting a dog. Finally, the time was right, and Lucky, a fluffy brown rescue pup, bounced into her life. She and Lucky quickly bonded, but the addition was not without its costs—from companion fares on flights, to some significant surprise vet bills. Fortunately, another round of planning confirmed Lucky was worth every penny.

A DIFFERENT KIND OF SURPRISE

Next, Elizabeth experienced a different kind of surprise, and another complication. Except this time, it was surprisingly *good* news! Her employer went public, and the company's stock price soared after its initial public offering. This has created substantial potential equity compensation for Elizabeth to manage.

Cue some additional financial planning. These days, when Elizabeth and I get together, we sometimes reflect on the past. But mostly, we talk about her future. Is remote work from a new location a possibility? Is there a dating app that doesn't suck? Maybe another furry friend for Lucky?

There are wrinkles as well, such as some anxiety about caring for her aging parents. Once again, we crunch the numbers and reaffirm the planning, so Elizabeth can do what she cares about today, while building for a promising future.

TAKING CARE OF YOUR CURRENT AND FUTURE SELF

Looking back, I'm so glad that Elizabeth and Steve purchased that pricey chef's dinner that brought us together so long ago. I hope Steve had the night of his life. For Elizabeth, I hope she looks back on the memory as fondly as I do.

I look back at that celebration as a reminder that financial planning is as much about now as it is about the future. Before Steve was gone, he and Elizabeth had traveled extensively to Hawaii, India, and Europe. They visited good friends, enjoyed special experiences, and dined well. I'm so glad they didn't decide to postpone their adventure into a future they never got to share. I remember this lesson as I advise other clients on their own balance between today and tomorrow.

With financial planning—and life, for that matter—you can carefully prepare for some moments; others are going to hit you blindside. By expecting a fair share of both, you can best plan for your money to bridge the inevitable vulnerabilities you'll encounter as you build, and sometimes rebuild, your circle of life. This is why a financial planning relationship means I must meet my clients wherever they're at in life, not where yesterday's timeline prescribed they should be. When life changes, money changes, and when money changes, life can change as well.

As for Elizabeth, I am amazed at the transformative path she has forged out of her experiences. She has dwelled in dark valleys, but emerged enlightened (even if she doesn't feel that way every day).

She has been a pioneer: boldly relocating to a new community and creating her own space there. She has sustained a career that has created unexpected prosperity, and added a beloved fur baby to her family. She has shown that resilience often comes with lifelong scars, and that it's okay to let them show.

Elizabeth, thank you for providing me with the opportunity to work with you these past years. Your grace, authenticity, and courage have taught me lessons I will continue to treasure myself, and share with others.

IN SUMMARY

- Financial planning is as much about now as it is about the future.
- With financial planning, you can carefully prepare for some moments but also protect yourself against those that take you by surprise.

THE DINING ROOM TABLE—WHERE A FAMILY MEETS AND WHERE YOU MEET YOUR FAMILY

Jeffrey J. Smith, CFP® CPWA® RMA® ChFC® CRPC®

I am Wolf's Dad and Karen's husband. Professionally, I am a managing partner and private wealth advisor, with more than 20 years of expertise in financial and wealth planning. Prior to forming OWL Private Wealth Advisors, I was a first vice president of wealth management at UBS, where I served not only as a wealth advisor but also in a leadership role for the Michigan Market. I am a graduate of the Eli Broad College of Business at Michigan State University and have completed post graduate coursework at The American College, Oakland University, The College for Financial Planning and, most recently, The University of Chicago Booth School of Business. When not in the office, I enjoy spending time with Karen and Wolf—skiing, playing golf, and cheering on the Michigan State Spartans.

"WOULD YOU BE open to sitting down with my grandparents to help them figure a few things out?"

That question from my friend and colleague George would be the start of a lifelong relationship that has taken me to places I never expected, with a family that is not my own.

MY YOUTHFUL FOLLIES

In the early 2000s, George and I worked together at a large national investment bank. Compared to George, I was a "seasoned" veteran in my mid-20s, who thought I'd seen it all in the four years since I'd gotten licensed.

Little did I know how little I knew. Then (and probably now), brokerage training meant heading to New York City and being thrown to the wolves. Financial service consisted of learning how to convince people to buy your financial products, because you supposedly knew things they did not. The internet had not yet taken over, there were no robo-advisors, and stockbrokers and day traders ruled the day. Like many aspiring college grads, I dreamed of a corner office and an enviable book of clients who were eager to entrust me with their life's savings.

Then I met George's grandparents, Frank and Mary J.

The Js were the parents of six children and 15 grandkids. Frank had served his country in the Korean War and eventually became a handyman. Mary was his loving wife, who had raised those six children to one day become parents of their own. The family was as close as could be, even after some had moved from Michigan to a warmer climate.

The first conversation about a family's finances is tricky. Sometimes it's easy, and sometimes it's like pulling teeth. This was a little of both. Frank had a harder shell than Mary, but once I cracked it, he was like the grandfather I never knew. One of my grandfathers had passed away before I was born, and the other when I was too young to have memories of him. I remember thinking to myself, "I wonder how my grandfathers would have acted if a strange young 'financial advisor' had visited their home to discuss their life's savings with them shortly after sitting down at their dining room table?"

In that context, I believe Frank was actually pretty patient with me.

THE GRANDFATHER I NEVER HAD

I quickly learned Frank already knew how to spot when a financial product was more sizzle than steak. They'd been investing longer than I had been alive, buying stocks in companies they knew and liked. In the 1960s–1970s, this was not as easy as it is today. There were no phone apps or automated processes, and trading costs could eat you alive. But they did it anyway, to provide for themselves and their family when they were no longer around.

It took almost six months and multiple meetings at their dining room table, but eventually we began to trust one another. Over the next few years, we worked through the financial questions that concerned them the most. I visited with them regularly, and each time I enjoyed my time with them more than the last. Family photos watched over us from the wall next to the table, reminding me to take good care of the Js, no matter what my employer had tasked me to do.

LEARNING AND UNLEARNING

We learn from each new thing that happens in our lives. In this case, I learned about the Js and their lives, their family and what mattered the most to them. Every time I visited, there were new things to address and questions to follow up on. Frank and Mary never thought about the day-to-day ups and downs of the company stocks they owned or followed. They thought in terms of, "What is best for our family?" They asked, "What makes the most sense for our goals and dreams?" They wondered,

"How can we leave our kids and grandkids in a better place than when we started?"

This was Frank and Mary's gift to me: There was no "Buy this, sell that," or "Do this because so and so says to do it." Instead, I unlearned what I'd been trained to do, and learned from them what financial planning really was, and how to truly help people succeed. Our time spent together also showed me what I would want to have in place for my own family one day, and how I would like to be thought of when I am no longer around.

CELEBRATING A GREAT MAN

As life goes on, we ultimately lose those we care about, and soon I would lose Frank. I attended his funeral and sat in the back of the church, not really making myself known to his family and friends. It was not only a celebration of a great man, it was the first time since I had started in financial services that I had lost a client, or friend, or whatever you want to call it.

It was hard. I cried and was sad, even though I knew he had lived a great life and left a beautiful legacy with his wife and family. I eventually gave my condolences, and left to return to my day at the office, feeling a quiet gratitude for the sun in the sky.

NEXT STEPS

I soon visited Mary to discuss all the things we had done up to that point, and to focus on her concerns moving forward.

We learned about Frank's veteran benefits, and how we could secure them to help her when she most needed it. Her daughters would often join us at that same dining room table in their childhood home, and we would work with them too, to protect the funds Mary and Frank had worked so hard to accumulate. We would also laugh, cry, and talk about what a great man their dad was. And how much Mary was enjoying her family, and her grandkids, and her great grandkids.

Over the course of the next few months, I also began to hear from the Js' children about their own lives. Little by little, we had conversations like I'd had with their parents about the things that kept them up at night, the things that excited them, and what their dreams were for the future.

FAMILY TIES

The call came one day, unexpectedly, even though we all knew it was inevitable. Mrs Mary J had gone to be with the love of her life. She was a strong, smart, witty, and funny lady. I miss our time together at her dining room table.

As we celebrated her life, I felt like I was honoring the life of my grandmother. It may seem crazy to you reading this, but I felt that way. Years later, it wasn't a surprise when my own grandmother passed, and the daughters of Mrs J came to support me at the memorial.

As the years moved on, I eventually started an independent financial practice with a good friend of mine. Thankfully, Mr and Mrs J's family have continued to grant me the gift of helping three generations of their family navigate through their life events: retirements; cross-country moves; births and next-generation births; weddings and funerals. Each time I see and speak with any of the Js, it takes me back to that dining room table where I first met the patriarch and matriarch of them all.

The work we do for each other matters. The decisions we make together at the dining room table have an impact—not only that day, but for decades to come. Thank you for teaching me that, Frank and Mary J.

IN SUMMARY

- A financial advisor can feel as much like a family member as a professional service provider.

ABOUT THE EDITOR
AND CURATORS

Shanna Due—Editor

 Shanna Due is an Accredited Financial Counselor (AFC®), co-founder of The Due Collaborative consulting group and Due Financial.

Whether working with her financial planning clients, consulting through The Due Collaborative, or volunteering in support of her local community and military families, Shanna is committed to seeing individuals use their capital, time, treasure, and talents to create a life focused on making an impact in the world around them. She has served as a board member, an advisor, seminar leader, and coach to hundreds of participants ranging from teens to retirees.

Shanna currently lives in Williamsburg, Virginia with her husband, two children, and rescue pup. In her free time, you can find her on the sidelines cheering on her children, searching for a hidden mountain lake, or reading a book on her latest obsession.

Taylor Schulte—Curator

TAYLOR SCHULTE, CFP® is the founder of Define Financial, a fee-only financial planning firm dedicated to helping people over age 50 lower taxes, invest smarter, and retire with confidence. He's also the co-founder of Advisors Growing as a Community (The AGC) and host of the Stay Wealthy Retirement Show, a Forbes top 10 podcast. Schulte was named as the #3 top independent financial advisor by Investopedia in 2021. His contributions are regularly featured in Kiplinger, Business Insider, and CNN.

Justin Castelli—Curator

JUSTIN CASTELLI IS the founder of RLS WEALTH, a registered investment adviser based in Fishers, Indiana and a co-founder of Advisors Growing as a Community (The AGC). More importantly, he is a husband and a father to three boys. As a CFP® practitioner, he focuses on helping clients identify their passions in life and make them the focus of their financial lives. Justin is also the creator of the All About Your Benjamins blog and podcast and recently launched a new creative effort called PRST. Passion is the driver behind all of Justin's endeavors and experiments in life, and he is inspired to help more people find their passions and purpose in life.